# I'm Fired

*A unique approach
to rebuilding your life*

## *About the Author*

Dr Eileen L Berman, a licensed psychologist, has practised clinical and corporate psychology in both the US and Australia. She has consulted with hundreds of senior and middle-level managers in a wide range of organisations, from family-owned businesses to large, multinational corporations.

Prior to her tenure in Australia, she was a psychologist at the Fallon Clinic, Worcester, Massachusetts; a consultant to Worcester Academy a private preparatory school in Worcester, Massachusetts and Adjunct Professor of Education and Psychology at Assumption College Graduate School and Worcester State College.

For ten years, Dr Berman wrote a monthly column on stress and productivity for *Business Digest* and also published the CEO *Growletter*. The *Growletter* focused on creating employee optimisation and was read throughout the US, Australia, Japan and India. At present, she writes a monthly column for *Industrial Management* magazine. Dr Berman's second book, *Building Productivity: 18 Blueprints for Success,* has just been published by Authority Press in Alpharetta, Georgia.

Dr Berman was also recognised by the Editorial Board of Biographical Publications of St Ives, Cambridgeshire, England as one the foremost women of the 20th century.

# I'm Fired

*A unique approach
to rebuilding your life*

*Eileen Berman, Ed.D.*

BLACKHALL
*Publishing*

This book was typeset by Artwerk for

**BLACKHALL PUBLISHING**
26 Eustace Street
Dublin 2

Ireland

e-mail: blackhall@tinet.ie

© Eileen Berman, 1999

ISBN: 1 901657 48 5

*This book was first published in the USA by*
*Engineering & Management Press*
*A division of The Institute of Industrial Engineers*
*25 Technology Park*
*Atlanta*
*Norcross*
*GA 30092-2988*
*USA*

A catalogue record for this book is available
from the British Library.

All rights reserved. No part of this publication may
be reproduced, stored in a retrieval system or transmitted
in any form or by any means, electronic, mechanical,
photocopying, recording or otherwise, without the prior,
written permission of the publisher.

This book is sold subject to the condition that it shall not,
by way of trade or otherwise, be lent, resold, hired out,
or otherwise circulated without the publisher's prior consent
in any form of binding or cover other than that in which it is published and
without a similar condition including this
condition being imposed on the subsequent purchaser.

Printed in Ireland by
ColourBooks Ltd

## *Table of Contents*

*Preliminary Notes* ............................................................. ix

SITE VISIT 1: *The Unthinkable* ................................................ 1

SITE VISIT 2: *Reality Confronted* ........................................... 11

SITE VISIT 3: *"What Did I Do Wrong?"* ................................. 25

SITE VISIT 4: *"Who Am I?"* ..................................................... 35

SITE VISIT 5: *Your Choice – Letting Go* ................................ 47

SITE VISIT 6: *Moving On* ........................................................ 55

SITE VISIT 7: *Taking Control* .................................................. 69

SITE VISIT 8: *From Danger To Opportunity* ......................... 77

*Final Notes* ........................................................................ 85

# *Preliminary Notes*

MERGERS, ACQUISITIONS, AND DOWNSIZING are rampant in business today. As companies struggle to remain competitive, employees face the prospect of losing their jobs. Reports continue to tell us of the growing number of employees who have either been given early retirement or have been discharged from their positions.

Are you one of the army of the newly unemployed? If so, your ability to cope, to function optimally, to enjoy your life, may be in a state of upheaval in the current business scene. You never thought it could happen to you? Well, join the ever-growing club. No matter what the circumstances, you may feel that you have somehow been at fault. All the talking in the world doesn't dispel that feeling of guilt that you must have done something wrong. Feelings of security – about yourself, your ability to earn a living, your future – are in a meltdown. As a result, your recovery from the shock of losing your job may take longer than necessary.

In times like these, it is normal to feel a great sense of loss; you may even feel depressed. In order to pull yourself out of the doldrums and get on with your life, you need to find a way to regain some measure of stability so that you can replenish your confidence in yourself. This is vital before you go out and find another job – the right job. If you don't pull yourself together, you will jeopardise the very result you want so badly: to get back in the workforce and re-establish your identity as a responsible, earning, worthwhile individual.

If you are to move ahead with your life, it is important for you to reconstruct your 'emotional house'. In this way, you will regain the self-esteem that was shattered when you received your P45. This book will show you how to make use of the tools you already have available for the work of reconstruction.

And what is your 'emotional house'? It is the emotional structure you have built through all the years of your life. It is instrumental in how you perceive and function in the world around you. When it is sturdy and strong, it keeps you safe, secure, and protected from too much stress. Its stability determines how well you respond to adversity. Losing a job is like an earth tremor that causes your emotional house to tremble and, possibly, to collapse.

When you experience an unusual amount of stress, not only is your emotional structure in jeopardy, but your physical structure as well. Body and mind work together. When either is excessively stressed, the other is affected. When you lose your job, your emotions are battered. Your sleep and your appetite are upset, which eventually takes a toll on you physically. To remedy this, you need to reconstruct your emotional house as quickly as possible so that it will stand firm and strong once again.

What tools will you need for this reconstruction? Tools such as communication and confrontation that you once used automatically seemed to disappear in the aftermath of your job loss. Those skills, along with others in your house kept you productive and emotionally sound, but with the shock of losing your job, chances are you're not using them now. The trauma you have undergone has driven them undercover. Yet you need these skills now more than ever. Nagging thoughts of guilt and self-doubt prevent you from feeling good about yourself and from recovering enough to begin to make progress in your life again.

If you are like most people, through the years you have probably built your emotional house without thinking. As a result of your experiences, the components are there for you to use. Sometimes you utilised them well, without even being consciously aware of doing so. But when you suffer a serious trauma, one that knocks you flat emotionally, you need to take a step back from the situation and reassess the materials that make up your emotional house.

In rebuilding it, you will reclaim the tools you need to lower your stress level. You will rediscover what you require to prepare the soil for your house so that it will stand firm without shifting. You will re-learn how to build a firm foundation, erect solid walls, and put on a strong and weatherproof roof, so that your house will not collapse when an ill-wind blows. When you're all done, you will have the key to a house that provides you with a sanctuary from stress and gives you the stability necessary to move on with your life.

Why is rebuilding this house so important to you? Because you, like millions of other people, are in a state of crisis. It is a crisis of self-confidence; and unless you regain your confidence, you will not be able to think clearly or to choose wisely.

The Chinese configuration for 'crisis' consists of two characters: 'danger' and 'opportunity'. It symbolises a crossroads – one route leading to recovery and another to continued suffering. Believe it or not, you have a choice as to which path you take. Right now you may not think you have any choice. All you see is danger. However, if you're willing to reconstruct your house, you will be able to reclaim the skills you already possess in order to pursue opportunity. If you choose not to make this effort, you will continue to walk down the path of danger.

The workplace today is fraught with anxiety as jobs continue to be eliminated. As companies downsize, merge, and are taken over, people have either lost their jobs or are worried about being unemployed. Because of the stress that accompanies job loss, many people do not take the time to reflect in order to turn danger into opportunity. They proceed in a panic to the first job offered which, many times, is not the right one. This keeps them in the danger zone. Before they know it, they have missed an opportunity to re-evaluate their lives and are, instead, involved in another unfulfilling and unrewarding experience.

Bob, the protagonist in our story, is faced with such a crisis. Given his emotional state and the financial needs of his family, what is he going to do? How is he going to handle this? Does he have the tools necessary to find opportunity rather than danger?

As you read about Bob, you may find yourself identifying with him regardless of your specific situation. You may be facing your own job crisis right now. As Bob learns how to rebuild his emotional house, you, too, will discover what you need to do in your own reconstruction. As Bob embarks upon his journey to self-discovery, you will begin your own journey as well.

Now, if you're ready to look within yourself and discover what you will need to make your emotional house stand firm and strong once again, you can move on to the construction site.

You do not have to bring safety glasses or overalls, but you will need a notebook and pencil. After each visit to the construction site, you will be asked certain questions. By answering them in your journal, you will find yourself moving through the project very effectively. And by reviewing your journal periodically, you will have the tools necessary to keep your emotional house strong. Everything else you will need for the task of recreating this all-important structure will be supplied in the following pages.

So get your notebook and your pencil and…let's go!

SITE VISIT 1

## *The Unthinkable*

IT WAS FRIDAY, TWO WEEKS AFTER the Christmas holidays, when the unthinkable happened. The way it happened would be etched in Bob's memory forever.

Bob was a 48-year-old executive with the Marter Corporation. He had been with the company for 25 years and was proud of the way his dedication and devotion to his work had paid off.

From the beginning Bob had been considered a rising star, and his career path bore witness to it.

That particular morning, at 8 o'clock, Bob was scheduled to attend a meeting with four other managers in his supervisor's office. When he arrived, however, no one was there but Harry, his supervisor. Bob was surprised since everyone usually appeared on time.

"Morning, Harry. Hey, where is everybody?" Bob asked, as he looked around the office.

Harry fidgeted in his chair and cleared his throat. "Oh, I called off the meeting."

Called off the meeting? Bob wondered why he hadn't been told. He was about to ask when he noticed Harry's nervousness. Harry's eyes looked everywhere but at Bob. His hands kept shuffling and rearranging the papers on his desk. Bob began to feel anxious. What was going on?

Harry stood up, looked down at his desk, and murmured, "Say, Bob, have you got a minute? I want to talk to you."

Alarm bells went off in Bob's head. For some reason, he had a sense of dread. He stood frozen, waiting for Harry to continue.

What was Harry saying? "Sorry...let go...we're consolidating...job being eliminated." Harry didn't look at him and seemed in a rush to get this over with. Suddenly, there was silence. Bob could not quite believe he had heard correctly.

"What did you say?" Bob asked with a stunned expression on his face.

"I'm sorry to be the bearer of bad news, Bob. Your job is being eliminated."

Bad news? My job being eliminated? These were words Bob had never imagined he would hear. He couldn't believe that they had been directed at him. For a moment, he wondered if it was some sort of sick joke. Harry had a weird sense of humour sometimes.

"You must be kidding, Harry." Bob tried to keep his voice from shaking.

"I'm afraid I'm not kidding," Harry still didn't meet Bob's eyes. "But look, it's really not that bad. You can take early retirement. You'll be well-compensated." The forced note of enthusiasm in Harry's voice made Bob feel sick.

Bob heard himself say, "But I don't want to retire," and wished he hadn't sounded so strained and upset.

Harry sat down slowly and pushed the papers around on his desk. He looked up and squared his shoulders as he quietly spoke the words Bob would never forget. "Then I'm sorry, Bob, but I'm afraid we'll have to let you go."

"You mean I have no choice?"

"I'm afraid not, Bob. That's just the way it is. We have to cut costs so we're consolidating throughout the company."

Bob's head swam. He was so disoriented that he couldn't feel much of anything, except numbness. His mouth was so dry that it hurt to swallow. He looked at Harry but couldn't really see him. Harry's voice seemed to come from far away. Bob thought he heard Harry say something like "three months in the outplacement department to look for another job". And then suddenly – with the falsely hearty words, "Good luck, Bob," and a brief, embarrassed handshake – it was all over. Just like that. A relationship of 25 years was ended. Just like that. In a couple of minutes, everything that Bob thought he was working for had ended.

Hardly thinking or feeling, Bob walked out of Harry's office and into his own. His heart racing, he closed the door and leaned against it, not knowing what to do. He simply could not believe it had happened to him. Not him. Sure, people were laid off in the firm, but not people like him. He was a star, an achiever. Bob stood motionless, hardly able to breathe, as he tried to digest what he had just been told.

– o –

In order to understand what a shock this was, you have to know a little bit about Bob. Bob, like so many people in the corporate world, was a 'sacrificer'. He sacrificed everything for the company: himself, his family, his feelings. He was willing to work hard, never questioning the demands made on him.

Actually, Bob really enjoyed his investment of time and energy because he had faith in the system. Of course, he missed not having more time to spend with his wife and children, but he felt that was the way life had to be if you were a guy on the way up;

and Bob was a guy on the way up. Bob believed in and identified with the corporation. He was certain that if he thought of the company first, he would be amply rewarded and both he and his family would ultimately be winners.

And it had happened that way. Bob started in Sales, and after a short while his territory was expanded. Soon he was promoted to Regional Sales Manager. As the years went by, Bob felt recognised as a significant part of the Marter Corporation. As a result, Bob was able to give his family more and more material things – a bigger home in an exclusive neighbourhood, new cars, and other luxuries he never thought he would acquire.

There was a price for all this, however. Bob worked long hours, including many nights and weekends. As he took on more responsibility, his time with his family dwindled. But Bob enjoyed the challenge of his work and the growing power he began to acquire within the organisation. So the cycle continued, with Bob always thinking of the company first. Among his peers he was known as 'the company man', and Bob took secret pride in being seen that way. What could be better for his career?

In time, Marter promoted Bob from Regional Sales Manager to National Director of Sales. His efforts were well compensated with both prestige and money. He felt he was an important member of the Marter Corporation. This was Bob's company. It belonged to him as well as to the shareholders.

Bob had never entertained a desire to work elsewhere. He thought that if he continued to perform well, one day he would become a member of the Board. Because of his total commitment to the corporation, and the corporation's apparent investment and belief in him, Bob was certain of his future. He assumed that he would be part of Marter until the time came for him to think about retirement. Given all this, what could possibly have happened to bring about this day?

Bob had been aware for quite some time that the business scene was changing rapidly. Competition, both foreign and domestic, had become more intense. Restructuring and company mergers were happening more and more frequently. Costs were out of control. Profits were down. Many companies were reducing headcount in order to make their dividend commitments.

# Site Visit 1: The Unthinkable

Anxiety began to haunt corporations as more and more companies downsized. White-collar as well as blue-collar workers were being dismissed. Managers and executives began to flood the labour market as businesses let people go in order to cut costs.

Bob saw it happening everywhere and knew it was happening at the Marter Corporation as well, but he was certain it would never happen to "people like me". He was as well-established in the company as the company was in him. His loyalty was unquestioned and his performance exemplary.

– o –

So, on that particular Friday in January, when Bob was told he was no longer needed, he did not believe what he had heard. As he walked slowly to his desk and sat down, his head reeled. This couldn't be happening. I must be dreaming. What did Harry say? Early retirement? Good grief, I'm only 48-years-old!

As Bob sat with his head in his hands, he felt numb. *I don't believe it. It must be a mistake. Harry must have made a mistake!* But the longer he sat, the more he knew it was no mistake. His number was up. *But why? There had to be a reason.* And then, hitting him in the gut were the words, *What did I do wrong?*

How could he find out the *real* reason for his termination? What had he done wrong? He thought that if he could find out what went wrong, he could fix it. Anxiously, Bob opened his office door and went looking for some of the members of the board. Maybe they could shed some light on this.

But nobody would see him. The senior executives made every effort to stay out of his way. When people couldn't avoid talking with him, their embarrassment and discomfort were painfully evident. Sure, they were sorry this had happened to good old Bob.

"But, you know, that's the ball game," they would say.

"Win a few, lose a few."

"If there's anything I can do…a letter or a phone call – just let me know."

"With your record, Bob, you won't have any trouble finding a job!"

By noon, Bob was exhausted. Alone and bewildered, he

returned to his office, closed the door, and slumped down into his chair. As fatigue settled in, the numbness suddenly left him and fear took its place. He felt sick, heavy and empty. He felt humiliated, ashamed, lost and guilt-ridden. He hadn't had an experience like this since his mother died when he was fifteen. Suddenly, Bob felt like a child again, alone and frightened. He put his head down on his desk and began to cry.

Eventually, Bob pulled himself together and began to empty his desk. He knew he had one more difficult task to complete before he left the office. He called his secretary in and told her he was leaving the Marter Corporation. *Why? What happened?* Bob told her his job had been eliminated. Polly couldn't believe it. She put her hands over her mouth as her eyes filled with tears. Suddenly, Bob found himself patting her awkwardly on the back and comforting her as she cried. He heard himself saying, "It'll be all right, Polly. Everything will be all right. I'm sure they'll find another place for you. Come on, we'll both be okay. Life will go on, you'll see."

He may have sounded strong and confident, but inside he felt weak and uncertain. He wasn't at all sure that life would continue for him. He couldn't believe he had found the strength to comfort Polly. He needed someone to comfort him.

Bob waited until most of the people on his floor had gone home before he left his office. He felt too miserable and ashamed to talk with anyone. Around 6 o'clock, when he thought it was safe, he went to his car as quickly as possible. He couldn't bear the thought of going home and telling his family he had failed them by losing his job. So, in order to clear his head, he decided to drive around a bit.

As he drove, he found himself thinking that he had somehow done something shameful. By the time he reached home, it was late and he had missed supper with his family. Bob was so haunted by guilt and humiliation that he was glad he didn't have to sit with his wife and children and pretend everything was all right.

Telling his wife he had had a bite to eat at the office and that he had work to do, he retired to his study and closed the door. He was glad to be alone. The energy he expended in order to appear 'normal' to everyone had drained him. He was not at all certain what he was going to do about his family. He was sure about only one thing: he was not ready to tell them what had happened.

For days, Bob kept the whole thing to himself. He couldn't sleep. He couldn't eat; he couldn't even look at himself in the mirror. Annie kept asking him if something was wrong, but he put her off by saying he was preoccupied with a very difficult project at the office.

Every day, as if everything were perfectly normal, Bob would get up at the same time and 'go to work'. In reality, he went to the outplacement department. He needed to begin to plan his future – a future with some other company. Bob felt as though he were in a daze and found that he couldn't concentrate on what people said to him. While he attended the outplacement sessions, he was distracted and removed from everything and everyone around him. Feeling demeaned and diminished at having to be part of these sessions, he paid very little attention.

As the days moved on, Bob began to withdraw from his friends and his family. He couldn't manage to talk to anybody, not even his wife, about his great disgrace. He was devastated by the thought that he had let them all down, that he had failed Annie and the kids. He couldn't believe that all their dreams were about to go up in smoke. Annie, sensing that something was not right, tried to cheer him up by talking about the vacation they had been planning for next summer. Bob just walked out of the room. There was not going to be any vacation.

Bob had not smoked for years, but suddenly he craved a cigarette. At night, he found it so difficult to relax that he began to take a drink before dinner, then more wine than usual with his meal, then a nightcap before bed, then two. For a while, the hazy numbness provided by the alcohol helped Bob blot out what had happened. He slept heavily but woke sweating in the night, unable to keep the fearful thoughts from running round and round in his head. During the day, because of his ever-increasing fatigue, he drank more and more coffee to keep awake.

Enmeshed in this cycle, Bob felt as if he were caught in some kind of vice. He felt trapped, unable to escape. He lost weight and looked worn and pale. Emotionally and physically, he was going downhill fast.

One day, nearly three weeks after his meeting with Harry, the fact that he had actually lost his job suddenly hit Bob. He had reached rock-bottom. His emotional pain was so great that he knew he had to talk about this with someone or he would burst. To whom could he talk? He certainly couldn't talk to Annie; he was too ashamed, too scared that he would see contempt in her eyes when she looked at him. What about George, his closest friend at the office? No, he couldn't do that; it would be too humiliating to tell George how frightened he felt. When Bob began to think about the possibility of sharing his feelings with someone, he realised that there wasn't anyone he really trusted. How could he unburden himself? What could he do?

Suddenly, Bob remembered a psychologist who had given a series of lectures on stress management at the Marter Corporation the year before. Bob had enjoyed those lectures. That psychologist seemed like the kind of guy he could talk to, kind of a comfortable person.

Why not? What had he to lose? Bob knew he had to do something, take some kind of action, in order to break out of this mental anguish that surrounded him. Before he could talk himself out of it, Bob picked up the telephone and dialed Dr Loring's number.

## *As we leave the site for the day, let's take notes*

❶ Was your history with your company similar to Bob's? Were you a 'sacrificer'?

❷ What was your immediate experience when you were 'let go'?

❸ Can you relate to Bob's sense of shame, guilt and fear? What were some other feelings you had?

❹ How did you tell your family and friends?

❺ What were your feelings when you told them?

❻ Did you tell someone *exactly* how you felt? Or did you just handle this superficially?

❼ And how are you feeling now…as you read this?

Site Visit 2

## *Reality Confronted*

WHEN BOB ENTERED THE WAITING ROOM of Dr Loring's office, he felt strangely detached. He could not quite believe he was going to see a psychologist. He had always thought that people who sought help with their problems from a psychologist or psychiatrist must be fairly crazy to start with. Up to this point, because he considered himself a strong, well-adjusted, 'normal' person, he had figured he could handle anything life dealt him without any help. Yet here he was. Did that mean he was losing his mind? He felt as if that was a pretty good possibility, and he questioned whether or not a psychologist would be able to help him put the pieces of his life back together again. Somehow, at this point, Bob didn't think he had any other choice.

Before long, Dr Loring opened the door and ushered Bob into his office, a pleasant, sunny room with comfortable chairs. English ivy and philodendron plants hung in the window, giving the room a warm, homey feeling. After they shook hands and introduced themselves, Dr Loring led Bob to a chair. The doctor settled himself in a rocker beside the desk opposite Bob. When Bob sat down, he found he wasn't as nervous as he had anticipated.

Dr Loring was a soft-spoken, kindly-looking man, grey at the temples, slightly balding, in his early sixties. He remembered Bob from the stress workshops he had given at Marter, so his first question was: "How are things going at work, Bob?"

Bob suddenly choked up. He felt his heart pounding, and he could barely get out the words. "Things aren't...aren't...going too well."

Dr Loring looked surprised and interested. "Not going well? What's wrong?"

Bob closed his eyes and whispered, "I guess...lots."

"Can you tell me about it?" Dr Loring said.

And, for the first time since that Friday at Marter, Bob told the story of how his boss Harry told him his services were no longer necessary.

"What was your reaction to this?" Dr Loring asked.

"My reaction? I couldn't believe it. In fact, I still can't believe it." Bob's voice began to rise. "Do you know how many years I've put into this company?"

"You sound bitter...and understandably so."

"Bitter? You bet I'm bitter. I can't believe they would just let me go!" Bob's voice broke and he began to cry.

Dr Loring rocked quietly, letting Bob empty out the pent-up hurt he had carried around inside him for weeks. Although Bob talked a lot, he couldn't bring himself to say he had been *fired*. He avoided the words in every way he knew how. But Dr Loring continually prodded him with more questions.

Finally, Dr Loring asked, "So what did they do to you, Bob?"

"Do to me? *Do to me?* They called it downsizing, but I feel as if I've been *fired!*" Bob yelled, unable to restrain himself.

With those words, Bob finally confronted his reality...his anger, his bitterness and his disbelief. With that outpouring, Bob took the first positive step in his journey from initial shock and depression to awakening, rebuilding and, ultimately, taking charge of his own life once again.

Dr Loring then asked Bob if he had told his family.

Bob admitted that he had not been able to bring himself to say anything to his wife and children. He felt so ashamed and frightened at what their reaction might be if they knew the truth that he had pretended that everything was all right. "Somehow, though," Bob said, "I think Annie knows something is wrong. She keeps asking if anything is bothering me. She keeps trying to cheer me up, talking about the trip we've planned for next summer. There isn't going to be a trip as far as I can see, but I can't manage to tell her so."

"Are you worried about your finances?"

"I'm damned worried. The company gave me a settlement that should last about a year, if I'm extra careful. But if I don't get a job soon, I'll be in trouble."

"Bob, you sound as if you think you're going to go through this alone. You keep saying *I* not *we*."

Bob was taken aback. "Well, I got us into this mess, so it's my job to get us out of it."

The doctor stopped rocking. "All alone?"

Bob paused. He was beginning to think and feel again. Why would he want to deal with such a downturn in his life alone?

Then he heard Dr Loring ask, "Do you think you're hiding your grief effectively?"

"Well, I'm certainly trying to," Bob said, "but it's not the easiest thing to do."

"Why do you want to hide how you're feeling?"

"I just can't bring myself to let anyone know what's happened. I can't even believe it myself. I keep thinking I'm going to wake up and find this has all been a bad dream." Bob rubbed his forehead. Lately, there always seemed to be a headache lurking just behind his eyes.

Dr Loring rocked gently for a moment. "So, by not divulging this to anyone – particularly, by not sharing it with your wife – you are hiding the truth from yourself as well."

Bob sat silent. When he finally responded, he said, "I hadn't thought of it that way." He continued very slowly, as if thinking out loud. "But I think perhaps you're right. Maybe if I don't have to talk about it, then maybe it's not really true."

Dr Loring made a brief note on the small pad in his lap. "Are you acting the same as usual around the house? Have you changed your behaviour at all?"

Bob thought for a minute. "Well, I guess I'm jumpier than usual. And I really don't talk too much. I seem to feel...I don't know, out of it."

"How about your sleeping and eating?" Dr Loring asked. "Any changes in those?"

Bob managed a lopsided, rueful grin. "Well, I really don't sleep very well," he said. "I toss and turn all night. My appetite's lousy. I've lost a few pounds, I guess, because my pants are a bit looser. Although I quit smoking five years ago, I'm back to two packs of cigarettes a day."

"What about alcohol and coffee?" queried the psychologist.

"Too much of both," said Bob without hesitation. "At night I need a few drinks to help me get to sleep; but then I wake up sometime in the early morning, and I can't fall asleep again. I just keep thinking...going round and round. So if I don't get extra caffeine during the day, I'm nodding off by lunchtime." He covered his face with his hands, and in muffled tones said, "Good Lord, I'm a mess."

"It's the typical vicious circle," said Dr Loring. "No wonder your wife keeps asking you how you feel. It sounds as if your behaviour has changed quite dramatically. She must be wondering if she has done something to cause this kind of change in you."

Bob sat bolt upright. "I never thought of what this might look like to Annie," he said slowly, "or that she might feel responsible. Frankly, I've had no other thought in my mind but that I lost my job and I've let her and the kids down. I don't know how to tell her."

Dr Loring leaned forward. His voice was serious, but warm.

"Bob, I understand what you're saying. You've suffered a tremendous loss. When you lose your job, or in your case your career, you feel as if your whole identity is gone. Your dreams for the future and your faith in yourself have been shattered. Your work with the Marter Corporation was really the center of your life; you built everything around it. Then somebody just took it all away from you, without any warning."

Bob swallowed hard and nodded in agreement. The psychologist went on. "What you're feeling now – loss, fear, shame, emptiness, disbelief, guilt – is called depression. You're so angry, yet you can't seem to express that anger in appropriate ways that would help you release that pressure building up inside you. Instead, you've chosen to deny what has happened. You truly cannot believe it. That's why you're not telling your family. If you put words to it, then it becomes real, and you won't be able to deny it any longer. That's why you hide your grief from your family. You also hide it from yourself. As you said, you hope you'll wake up and find it's all just a bad dream."

"You're right," Bob agreed. His fingers drummed nervously on the arm of his chair. "I don't really believe it all happened. Every morning I wake up, and for just a moment I believe this will all blow away and everything will be the way it was before. But every day I feel worse and worse." He looked up at Dr Loring, desperate for reassurance. "I think I may be losing my mind. Could that be true?"

"You're not losing your mind Bob," Dr Loring said emphatically. "What you're feeling is an acute reaction to loss. You've lost your job, and that's very serious because it's like losing your very self!"

"It's not as if someone died," said Bob, a note of irritation in his voice. "Why can't I just pull myself out of this?"

"Because in some ways," said Dr Loring, "it is as if *someone* died. That someone is you, the you that worked for Marter. All your eggs are in the work basket. You leave no room for much else in your life. So when you lose your job, it's like losing yourself, like dying. And that's quite a loss."

As Dr Loring spoke, Bob nodded in agreement. He related to everything the doctor said.

"How am I going to get over this?" Bob asked, leaning toward

Dr Loring. I can't go on this way indefinitely. I've got to start figuring out how I'm going to manage...how *we're* going to manage. We've got to get a plan to think about what comes next. But I can't seem to *do* anything." Bob's fingers trembled.

"Bob, you've done something already. You've begun to think in terms of *we* rather than *I*. That's going to give you a feeling of support, a feeling that you're not alone. Then, you did what many people would find very difficult – you came to my office. The reason you're here is that you need to talk about what happened so you can understand it and feel it. You see, in some ways, the emotional house that you live in has been shaken to its very foundation. I call it your 'emotional house', but it's an intellectual structure as well. Over the years, each person constructs a uniquely personal framework of emotions and attitudes. This is the emotional house in which he or she lives. If this house is on a firm foundation, embedded in good soil and solidly built, it will withstand all kinds of bad weather. But if there's a weakness in that structure, you have to do some rebuilding so you're protected from the elements once again. When your emotions are not free to handle the situation adequately, too much stress will cause the walls of your house to buckle and the foundation to tremble. So, the way you get better is to work on rebuilding your house."

"You want me to build a house?" Bob asked.

Dr Loring laughed. "Yes, figuratively speaking. You see, Bob, your emotional house is a special house. You actually have all the tools you need to rebuild your house already, but in your current state of shock, you've forgotten how to use them. I call this house the House of the 'Seven Cs' because each of its parts begins with a 'C', and there are seven major parts. You're going to rebuild this house so that you can learn to handle your stress, rather than have your stress handle you. If you can learn to use the key to unlock the door to this house, you'll come out of this experience much stronger and wiser. Are you willing to try?"

Bob thought for a moment, then shrugged. "I feel so rotten that I'm ready to do just about anything that will help me," he said. "At least I know I'm not crazy," he grinned. "What do I have to do first?"

"What's the first thing you have to do before you can build a house?" queried Dr Loring.

Bob thought for a moment. "I guess you have to find a site."

"Exactly. And the site – or the soil – has to be firm and compact, so that the house doesn't shift. You don't begin a building project on quicksand. Now, the site of this special house is called *courage*. That's the first big 'C'. Tell me, Bob, do you see yourself as courageous?"

"Well, I always thought I had what it takes, if that's what you mean," Bob said, "but right now I'm not so sure."

"Why is that?" Dr Loring asked.

"Because I feel so damn scared!" Bob's voice had become louder, but he felt a sense of relief when he realised he could admit his fear.

"Feeling scared doesn't mean you're without courage," said Dr Loring. "It simply means you're sensing danger, and losing your job certainly puts you in the danger zone. Don't you think fear is a normal response to such a loss?"

"When you put it that way, I guess it is," Bob replied, "but I'm not used to feeling afraid, and I don't like it very much."

"Most people don't like that feeling," Dr Loring agreed, "particularly men. In our society, men have been brought up to think they have to be brave and strong and fearless all the time. You know, 'be a man'! Even little boys are told, 'come on, act like a man'! Heaven forbid you show your feelings and cry, because if you do, you're not a man then, are you?"

Bob swallowed hard. He knew exactly what the doctor was talking about. He remembered so many instances in his childhood when he felt ashamed at feeling hurt and wanting to cry.

Through the haze of memories, Bob heard Dr Loring continue. "So you try to shut out fear and pretend it doesn't exist. When you grow up, you try to shut out frightening events by drinking too much or doing other destructive things. By not talking about something that scares you, you continue the pretence that it didn't happen. That's where courage comes in – our first 'C' in the House of Seven Cs."

"You mean talking about what happened is an act of courage?" Bob looked more interested.

"That's exactly what I mean. Talking, or communicating, is the first wall in our House of Seven Cs. It's one of the four walls in the house we're building. But you won't communicate unless you have the courage to face the reality of what has happened, and the reality of what you feel. Remember, our site – the soil on which the house stands – is *courage*. If you have the proper site, you can begin the construction of your House." Dr Loring rocked in his chair for a moment, elbows leaning on the arms of the chair and fingers tented together beneath his chin. "The foundation of a house situated on the proper site, of course, supports the whole structure. In this emotional house, the foundation is *confidence*. In order for you to begin to feel some sense of self-esteem – or confidence – you're going to have to use your courage to tell your wife and children what happened. How old are your children, Bob?"

"My son, Eric, is eighteen. He'll be going to college next year. My daughter, Alicia, is fourteen. They're both excellent students – into music and athletics. Kind of all around kids. You know, kids you can really be proud of."

"Then your task of communicating and rebuilding your confidence as a husband and father will be much easier than you imagine," Dr Loring said with a knowing look. "You have forgotten your most important assets: your wife and children. Let's start putting in the foundation of your house by telling them what happened and see how they'll react. And that brings us to the first two walls of your house. When you have courage and confidence in place, you can begin building the walls: first, *communication* then *confrontation*. It takes courage to stop denying what is so painful to admit, Bob. But the reality of the situation has to be faced, and the sooner you do it, the faster your confidence will return. Do you think you're ready to confront reality and communicate how you feel?" Dr Loring was speaking very seriously now.

"Well, I don't think I can stand feeling this way much longer," Bob answered. Then, almost in a whisper, he said, "Will I feel better if I talk about it?"

The psychologist nodded his head slowly. "Yes, you will, in time. To be honest, Bob, I think it's going to hurt like hell to talk about it. But, you have to go through that hurt, if you want to feel better eventually. You see, Bob, you're in a state of crisis. That's another 'C' word. I'm sure you know what a *crisis* is."

Bob shrugged his shoulders. "Well, if this is a crisis I'm in, I can tell you it hurts."

"Of course it does," Dr Loring said, tapping his pen on his pad, "one way to think of a crisis is as a crossroads. And the House of Seven Cs is always tested on a crossroads. In the Chinese tradition, the configuration representing crisis consists of two parts coming together: *danger* and *opportunity*. In other words, in a crisis, there are always two elements you must face: danger and opportunity. A crisis is a time in life which forces you to make a *choice*, the third wall of your house. You must decide which path you will take. *Change*, the fourth wall of your house, always occurs during a crisis. Something usually changes, which brings on the crisis. So, by definition, a crisis is a very stressful time because change – whether good or bad – brings stress. Holding this whole structure together is the roof, *control*. Your ability to control your emotional house is vital to your functioning effectively. Am I making this clear?" Dr Loring asked, noticing that Bob looked puzzled.

"I...ah...think so," Bob said hesitantly.

"Well, it's a lot to take in at first. We'll get to it all in much more detail in future sessions," Dr Loring said, making notes on his pad. "Meanwhile, let's concentrate on what it is to be in a crisis. A crisis is a very painful time because in order to move forward, you have to leave what's comfortable, safe, and familiar for something you're not quite sure of. It brings about change. That's another reason you need courage; so you won't be afraid to take a different road in order to get on with your life. You see, Bob, if you're in crisis, you have to confront the issue that's pushed you into the danger zone; the issue that's central to the crisis. Are you ready to do that, Bob?"

Bob sat up a little straighter, squared his shoulders ever so slightly, and responded, "If I understand you correctly, if I want to get back to feeling okay again, then the answer is yes."

"Good," Dr Loring said. "Now, what do you think your first act of courage must be?"

Bob responded thoughtfully. "I guess I'm going to have to tell Annie and the kids."

"Exactly," said the psychologist. "So now you're beginning to prepare your building site, which is *courage*. Courage is not easy to come by. You have to gird yourself to forge ahead when the going is rough. But if your emotional house is going to stand firm, proper soil is necessary. You're also beginning to put in the foundation and two of the walls of the house. One wall is *communication* and another is *confrontation*."

Bob frowned slightly. "Confrontation sounds like a negative word to me," he said. "Annie always tells me she doesn't want to have a 'confrontation' about this or that, and she usually means an argument or a fight."

"That's one meaning," agreed Dr Loring with a smile. "But in the House of Seven Cs, *confrontation* is positive. It simply means facing the issue head on. If you face the issue and communicate appropriately, you'll start to reduce the stress that's building up inside you. Stress increases when you pretend that certain facts don't exist and you refuse to acknowledge or talk about them."

"And the issue here is that I lost my job." Bob's voice, although still quiet and sad, was a little firmer than it had been earlier when he had first acknowledged that he was fired.

Dr Loring nodded. "That's what you must confront. When you have the courage to say it out loud, you hear it. When you say it to someone else, they hear it. Then it's real. You have communicated what you fear most. You have let someone know what happened to you. And you have also told yourself."

"And I guess that's why I need courage," Bob said.

Dr Loring leaned forward. "You need courage to face your own fears. That's the only way to get rid of them. By doing this, you begin to turn down the pressure valve on your emotions. It's the building up of pressure that is causing you to lose sleep and not eat very well. It's the pressure that is causing you to smoke and drink too much. So by building this House of Seven Cs, you'll reduce the pressure and begin to take charge of your life once again. And that is how you will begin rebuilding your *confidence*, the foundation of your house."

"It sounds almost too easy," mused Bob. Then his face fell. "But when I think about telling Annie, I know it's not easy."

"Why? What do you mean?"

"Because I feel as if I've failed her and the kids. They count on me for everything and I've let them down." Bob lowered his head and sighed, "I feel like a real loser."

"Bob, losers don't walk into my office," Dr Loring said. "It takes courage to face reality and talk about your problems. After

## Site Visit 2: Reality Confronted

all, I'm essentially a stranger, and you didn't know how I was going to react. Most people feel uncomfortable at the very thought of coming to see a person in my profession. They would rather live with their pain than take the chance of seeing a psychologist. So you see, Bob, you have more courage than you realise. That's why I think you're going to be a very good builder."

Bob grinned sheepishly. "Well, maybe I did show *courage* in coming here. But I still don't look forward to telling my wife," he added.

"Of course you don't," Dr Loring agreed, "but you grow by doing things that are painful to do but that you know are right. And while you will feel pain in the telling, you'll also begin the healing process. That's why *courage* is the soil. Without good soil, no matter how strong the foundation and the structure, the house will shift. So before you begin to build the actual house, you need to test the soil. Do you think you're up to it?"

"I'm going to find out." Bob met the psychologist's challenge by lifting his chin slightly and looking directly into his eyes.

"Sounds as if you have more courage than you realised." Dr Loring got up from his rocking chair, moved to his desk, and picked up his appointment book. "I'd like to see you next week, Bob, about the same time so you can continue working on building your house."

When Bob rose to leave, he realised his knees weren't shaking the way they had been when he walked in. He actually felt better, lighter, more in charge of himself, than he had felt in weeks. The mere fact that he had been able to say to someone, "I've lost my job," seemed to lighten him by removing a burden he hadn't even realised he had carried.

Bob took a deep breath. When he realised he was going to confront what had really happened and communicate his thoughts and feelings to Annie, his mouth grew dry and his heart raced. Although thinking about it made him anxious, he also felt a sense of relief at the thought of unburdening himself to his family. What a strange mixture of emotions!

The site for his construction – *courage* – was being prepared; and two walls of the House of Seven Cs, *confrontation* and *communication*, were about to be erected. He was also helping prepare the foundation. If Dr Loring were right, once Bob summoned up the *courage* to tell his family, his *confidence* would rise.

The numbness and daze of the past few weeks lessened. Bob was suddenly more aware of himself and others. As he left the office building, he looked up and saw that the sun was shining. It was the first time since his interview with Harry that he had noticed the sun. Bob felt ready to begin.

## *As we leave the site for the day, let's take notes*

1. How did you confront the reality of your dismissal?

2. Have you been able to bring yourself to tell the people who are closest to you that you have lost your job? If not, why not? Here you must delve into yourself in a way that helps you uncover your motivations. Find specific instances when you chose not to disclose your feelings and figure out why you chose that path.

3. Can you identify with the feelings of loss that Bob had: fear, shame, emptiness, disbelief, and guilt?

4. How have you begun to show courage in your daily life so that you can dispel those feelings?

5. Describe your behaviour at home immediately after you lost your job. Is it different now?

6. To whom can you communicate your deepest feelings associated with your loss? Have you done so?

7. List some of your qualities that will ensure a firm foundation to your house. What have you done since the devastating news that has helped rebuild your self-confidence?

8. List some of the issues that you have confronted that have stood in the way of rebuilding.

9. Confront the issue of your health: Are you exercising? Are you eating properly? Are you seeing friends?

Site Visit 3

## *"What Did I Do Wrong?"*

The following week, Bob went to Dr Loring's office for his second appointment. He was slightly less anxious this time, now that the psychologist and his office were more familiar. As the two men settled into their chairs, Dr Loring asked, "Well, how was your week, Bob?"

In a voice that was heavy and sad, almost expressionless, Bob answered, "Well, I finally got up enough courage to tell Annie that I'd lost my job. After her initial shock, her first question was whether I was all right. That made me feel better. Then we talked for a while and decided to tell the kids together."

"How did it go?" Dr Loring asked.

"Well, it wasn't easy," Bob sighed. "We were sitting around the table, just finishing dinner, when I asked them to stay a bit. I said I had something very important to tell them. They seemed surprised and kind of uncomfortable. Eric wanted me to hurry up because he had a date." Bob chuckled. "Can you imagine his date was more important than my job?" Bob laughed.

"What about Alicia? Did she have a date, too?" Dr Loring asked, smiling.

"Not quite. Lucky, I guess. She just sat there watching and waiting. I think she sensed something pretty unusual was going on." Bob grew silent and paused for quite some time as he thought about that night.

"Then what happened?" Dr Loring asked, encouraging Bob to go on.

"Well, I guess I cleared my throat a few times. I really didn't know how to start. I was really dreading it. The kids looked at me as if I was going to tell them I had won the lottery, but it was just the opposite." Bob sat silent once again, shaking his head as if he were still in a state of disbelief. "Then I told them that the company had laid me off and I would have to get a new job."

"And how did they react?"

"Well, at first they didn't believe it. Then they wanted to know exactly what had happened. I told them as well as I could and tried to reassure them that we were going to come out all right."

Dr Loring slowly rocked back and forth as he waited for Bob to continue.

"Eric wanted to know if he would be able to go to college. Then Annie piped up and wanted to know if we would have to sell the house. And Alicia...that was the toughest of all. She got so angry saying that she would never leave her school even if we moved."

"So each of them had different concerns, but, in the end, did they pull together?"

Bob nodded, seemingly relieved. "Luckily, they did, and I sure felt better. After I reassured them that we were going to make it, the kids got up and left, but Annie and I stayed and talked for a long time."

Dr Loring was interested in Annie's reaction. He knew that without her support, this could be a rocky road for Bob and the family. It would be bumpy enough anyway, but Annie was needed to calm the situation down. "How exactly did your wife react after the initial shock?"

"My wife was very angry," Bob replied. "In fact, I don't know when I've seen her so furious."

"Why was she angry?" Dr Loring asked.

"She was angry at me for not sharing this with her right away. She felt left out, unimportant – and started to cry. I felt terrible. I tried to tell her that I felt so guilty about losing my job that I just couldn't bring myself to tell her. It had nothing to do with her being unimportant. In fact, it's because she is so important, that I didn't want to have her disappointed in me. She kept saying that she couldn't possibly feel that way, that she has complete faith and trust in me." Bob's voice broke when he said this and he remained silent for a while.

Finally, Dr Loring said quietly, "Sounds as if your wife is in this with you, Bob."

"You're right and I needed to hear that."

Dr Loring continued to query Bob about Annie. "Is she angry at what happened?"

"Hell yes!" Bob said, "She's very angry! She feels they're unappreciative, and so on. You name it, she said it."

"But, with all this, she's being supportive of you?" Dr Loring asked.

"Absolutely!" Bob answered quickly and leaned forward slightly. "In fact, I'm amazed at how well she and the children are actually taking it. They all seem to think I got a very raw deal from Marter."

"That must feel good to you," Dr Loring said. "Does their attitude alleviate that sense of guilt and shame you were feeling?"

"Not really," admitted Bob. "I just cannot get out of my mind that I must have done something terribly wrong or they wouldn't have let me go just like that."

Dr Loring raised his eyebrows. "You did something wrong?"

"Of course," said Bob. "Why else would it have happened? And why else would I be here?"

The psychologist drew a deep breath and settled more comfortably into his rocking chair. "Okay," he began, "you remember that confrontation is one of the walls of the emotional house, don't you?" Bob nodded in agreement. "Well, you started building that wall when you told your wife and children, but we need to do more work on that wall today. Let's confront the issue of *What Did I Do Wrong?* Tell me, Bob, how much of yourself did you put into the company?"

Bob grimaced. He looked anything but happy. "You should ask my wife that question," he said. "That's one of the biggest causes of Annie's anger and bitterness. She used to say she was married to Marter! All those years when the children were little, and now that they're teenagers, I was hardly ever around. I was either travelling or at the office. I gave my whole life to that company. Early morning breakfast meetings that got me out of the house before the family was up. Dinner meetings that got me home after Annie and the kids were asleep. I travelled constantly. Whenever the company called, I jumped. As a result, I missed most of my kids' growing-up years. And the times when my wife was under a lot of stress for one reason or another, I wasn't there for her either."

Dr Loring nodded. "It sounds as if you made a choice early on to serve your company first, even before yourself and your family."

"You'd better believe it," Bob agreed. "There was never any question who came first. Annie knew when we got married that I was a company man. And now I'm let go in a major downsizing...as if I'm insignificant. That's why my wife is so bitter. She feels we sacrificed for nothing." Bob's voice had begun to rise as he spoke.

"How about *you?*" Dr Loring asked. "Are you still bitter?"

"I'm angry as hell!" Bob retorted without a moment's pause. "This is what I get after all these years! Out on the street! This isn't exactly how I planned my life. I'm 48-years-old and have been with one company all my life. What am I going to do? Where am I going to go?"

"Well," replied the psychologist calmly, "if you feel you are at fault in this, it's going to be very difficult for you to go anywhere at all. So let's talk about what you think *you* did wrong."

"That's just it," said Bob. He smacked his fist against his knee again and again. "I don't *know* what I did wrong and no one at that company will talk to me about it."

"Have you had performance reviews?" Dr Loring asked.

"Of course, and they've always been outstanding," Bob replied. "That's how I got to be a manager, and then National Sales Director."

Dr Loring tented his fingers together in a gesture that was becoming familiar to Bob. "Then you rose through the ranks because of your superior ability and performance, is that right?"

"Absolutely," Bob said firmly.

"Then how could you be guilty of poor performance?" Dr Loring asked.

"That's what I just can't put together," Bob said, unconsciously beginning to strike his knee with his fist again.

Dr Loring looked at him intently. "Bob, you know we met originally at the Marter Corporation when I was giving a series of seminars on stress. Well, I do that all over the country. I work with executives, managers and supervisors. As a result of my experience, I'm pretty much aware of what goes on in the inner workings of companies. Right now, it's pretty tough to maintain the bottom line. So the people in control have to do things which may be unpalatable...not only to the employees but even to them. In the long run, they have to satisfy the shareholders.

Bob looked puzzled. "I don't get it. What do you mean?"

Dr Loring explained. "I mean that in order to keep a company vital and growing, sometimes the people in charge have to take drastic measures. When a company is weakened...for whatever reasons...downsizing becomes necessary for the company's survival. And many times good people...people like yourself...people who contributed over the years to the company's growth...are discharged."

But why *me*? Why did they let *me* go?"

"I can assure you it's not because you didn't have a good track record, or that you did anything wrong. It's beyond that. It's a question of economics. 'How can we consolidate? Where can we save money? Who can fit into the new culture?' That's the thinking in corporations today."

Bob then said in a voice that revealed his hurt and bitterness, "But why was *I* let go? Why wasn't *I* the one chosen to stay and help renew the company?"

"I guess that's one of the things that's so unfair about life," said Dr Loring. "Why were *you* asked to leave and someone else allowed to stay?"

Dr Loring rocked for a few moments before he spoke again. "Companies have their rationale. It always comes down to the bottom line. It's a tough world out there. Highly competitive."

Bob said wryly, "I was part of that scene all my life. So many times I let people go...good people...because we had to make the numbers. I never thought I would get caught in that web. I was too good, too valuable to the company to be let go."

"Unfortunately," commented the psychologist, "whether or not you get caught in the web has very little to do with how good you are. What's important to the company is how it can stay competitive, and to do that, a business has to get lean. Unfortunately, many good people are let go to accomplish that goal."

"But wouldn't you think someone would have stepped forward and spoken in my favour after all I did for that company?" asked Bob. He couldn't keep a note of pleading out of his voice. "When I look back at that, when I think about all the guys who were supposed to be my friends, my colleagues...that's what really hurts."

Dr Loring shook his head slowly. "In this type of situation, Bob, everybody's scrambling to save his own job."

"How do you know that?" Bob looked up sharply.

"Because that's what always happens in times of downsizing," said the psychologist. But let me tell you...no one is safe in this type of environment...no one. Not even Harry, your old boss. He may find his day may come, too."

Bob looked uncertain, but also relieved. "Then you don't think it was anything *I* did? I didn't give them some reason to let me go?"

Dr Loring smiled slightly. "When you confront the issue this way, what do you think? Given your record, do you think it was something you did?"

Bob thought for a minute, then looked up at Dr Loring with sudden understanding. "When I look at it like that," he said, "I guess not. The company was losing money. We were ripe for takeover, and downsizing was the solution management decided upon. Given all that, I guess I drew the short straw. If you look at it that way, it wasn't my fault. There really wasn't anything I could have done to change things."

Dr Loring nodded. "That's what it means to be a victim of circumstances, Bob. But the question you need to consider is, *how long are you going to remain a victim?*"

"Do I have a choice?" Bob asked ruefully.

"Yes, you do have a choice. You can choose to be in control of your life, or you can let the events in your life control you. As a matter of fact, getting back to that house we're building – *control* is the roof of the House of Seven Cs. Before we get to the roof, however, we have to do some groundwork. We have to make sure the foundation on which the House stands is substantial, so that it won't crack under pressure. That foundation is what some people call self-esteem. I call it *confidence.*"

Bob listened intently as the doctor continued. "Confidence and courage are the most important and basic 'Cs' of the House of Seven Cs. In order to find out about that foundation, to ascertain how strong or how weak it is, you have to have the courage to step back a bit and discover who you really are. Who is this person in whom you need to have confidence? And to do that, we'll need to talk a bit about your past. We'll find out who you think you are, and we'll talk about where you came from, your family life, your childhood and your hopes and dreams for the future. You see, Bob," Dr Loring leaned forward again to hold Bob's eyes with his own, "that's where your confidence is created. It comes from your past, your achievements, your view of yourself. That's how you build the foundation of your emotional house. So that will be the topic for our next session, okay?"

"Sounds a bit scary, but I'll go along with it," Bob said.

"Sometimes it is scary to look at yourself. And that's why you need courage – because until you look, you'll never be free to live your life with a strong sense of freedom and choice. In fact, you've begun to take some very significant steps in that direction already." With a change of tone, Dr Loring asked, "How do you think your house is going so far?"

Bob grinned. "Well, it's pretty interesting. I certainly am beginning to see things differently."

"That's the whole idea," Dr Loring said. "I'll look forward to seeing you in a week then."

As Bob walked to his car, he realised that his step was lighter and brisker than it had been for weeks.

*What's happening? Am I getting a handle on things?*

He certainly felt better – not completely out of the woods, but definitely less stressed. He was eating better and getting more sleep than he had in the weeks before he told Annie. As he drove his car out of the car park, he thought he'd stop at the outplacement office and see if anything had come in for him. It was the first time in weeks that Bob hadn't felt ashamed to go there. Something good was, indeed, happening.

## *As we leave the site for the day, let's take notes*

❶ Have you got to grips with your own sense of guilt as to what you think you did wrong?

❷ What was the scenario at your company prior to your being dismissed?

❸ Give some examples of how you showed courage during this time. How are you showing courage now?

❹ Are you eating better? Sleeping better? Are you exercising regularly?

Site Visit 4

## *"Who Am I?"*

BOB SETTLED DEEPER INTO HIS favourite chair in Dr Loring's office. He always felt comfortable and safe within these walls. Today, they were going to talk about Bob's background, his beginnings. Dr Loring had said that in order to make sure of the firmness and strength of the foundation on which his house was being built, they would need to explore Bob's past.

Where did he come from? Who were his parents? Did he have any brothers and sisters? What was his early life like, both academically and socially? What had been his dreams, his goals? What had he hoped to accomplish? And, ultimately, given his history, how did he view himself? Bob had thought quite a bit about himself during the week since his last meeting with the psychologist, and he found himself remembering faces and events he had not recalled for years. Now, in response to Dr Loring's encouraging look, he began.

"I was the fourth child in a family of eight. There were two older brothers, a sister, then myself. I was followed by two younger sisters and two more brothers."

"Quite a sizeable family," Dr Loring commented. "Where did your parents grow up?"

"Well, my father's family had come here from Poland and my mother's family came from Germany. My parents were both born here in England, though – in Manchester."

"What did your father do for a living?" Dr Loring asked.

"My father left school at the age of fifteen to go to work and help his family," Bob replied. "He was a factory worker all his life. When we were kids, he worked long, hard hours to support us and we didn't see much of him. My mother stayed at home and took care of all us kids." Bob fell silent for a moment, deep into his past memories and feelings. Dr Loring remained quiet as well, waiting for Bob to continue. "My two older brothers were really the stars of the family," Bob went on. "They were outstanding students all the way along and good athletes, too. John played football in secondary school and Tom played rugby. They both got full scholarships to Cambridge and did very well there. Both of them are doctors now and very successful."

"What about you?" asked Dr Loring. "You were the third son, almost a middle child, if you look at that whole family constellation. How did you feel in that position? How did you feel about your brothers and sisters?"

Bob thought for a moment, but he knew the answer to these questions – he'd had to focus in upon them during the past week. "I guess I felt like the typical middle child most of the time, squeezed between two halves of a sandwich." Bob laughed and then turned serious. "I didn't feel like part of the older kids, but I didn't want to be seen with the younger kids either. I felt out of it, really. On my own most of the time, if you know what I mean. I looked up to my older brothers, of course. I always did well in school and in sports, but I was never a star, like Tommy or John. My father and my teachers kept comparing me to them. I really got sick of hearing 'Why can't you be more like Johnny?' or 'Tom wouldn't have missed that shot'." Bob grinned ruefully, hoping he didn't sound like a whiny, bitter little boy.

Dr Loring nodded sympathetically. "You must have felt as if you were constantly reaching and never quite getting there."

"Yeah," Bob said, surprised that the doctor could sum up his feelings so accurately. "That's exactly how I felt. In fact, I wanted to go to Cambridge like my brothers. John and Tom encouraged me to apply and I did, but I didn't quite make it. After my freshman year, I had the chance to transfer to Cambridge but I decided to stay put."

"Why was that?" asked Dr Loring.

"Well, to tell you the truth," Bob said, "I missed Tom and John, but at the same time I sort of liked being out from under their shadow. I liked being in a place where no one knew them. I felt like my own person for the first time. It felt great not being compared to my brothers. So I decided to stay where I was."

Dr Loring made a brief note on his pad. "Tell me, Bob," he said, "when you did well in sports or in your studies, how did your father react?"

"Unless I was perfect, he would usually tell me I hadn't done quite well enough," Bob said. "Oh, I'm sure he was proud of me, but he never really paid that much attention to me. Whenever I brought home a report card, he would look for perfection. I'd have a card full of As and maybe a couple of Bs, and Dad would say, 'What happened here? Why wasn't this an 'A'?' I'd find myself getting defensive, trying to explain that the course was really tough, or I'd worked really hard; but he'd just shake his head and say, 'Bobby, you can do better than that'."

Bob was surprised at how vivid this memory was, and how painful. He shrugged and waved a hand dismissively. "So I never felt he was pleased with me; I never felt I did things well enough for him. Remember, my two older brothers got straight As quite easily and they were star athletes. He constantly held them up to me as an example."

"So in many ways you must have felt like an 'also-ran'," Dr Loring suggested quietly.

"I sure did," Bob said.

"And in order to establish yourself as an individual in your own right, you decided to go to a different college. How about choosing your career? What made you decide go into business?"

"Well," Bob said, "I decided to do something I knew John and Tom wouldn't do. They were both in medical school. So I chose business."

Dr Loring nodded. "What did you hope to accomplish in a business career?" he asked.

Bob answered without hesitation, "I wanted to be a member of the board or a director of a company – eventually president and CEO."

"Nothing else would do?" the psychologist asked with a tiny smile.

"Evidently not," Bob said, returning the smile. "That was my goal when I was with the Marter Corporation, and it still is my goal. When I ask myself what I want to do, that's what I always come up with."

"So, even though you chose a different college and a different career from theirs, your brothers' successes still drove you," Dr Loring leaned forward slightly in his rocking chair. "You never really did get out from under them, did you, Bob? Even to this day, you've never really stopped competing with John and Tom for your father's approval."

"I don't see that at all," Bob said rather perturbed. "My father's been dead a long time."

"All the more reason to punish yourself," the psychologist said. "Many times a ghost can be more powerful than a living person. Trying to win praise from your father when he's been dead for years, that's pretty self-defeating, wouldn't you say?"

Bob sat silent.

After a long pause, Dr Loring continued. "Bob, do you begin to sense why you were reeling when you lost your job? And why you've been a workaholic all your life?"

"Well, if being a workaholic means I worked hard to reach my goal, then yes, you're right." Bob's tone had become defensive and a bit combative. "But when Marter let me go, everything I'd been working for was suddenly gone. Of course I was reeling!"

"Did you think this was proof that you really *weren't* as good as your brothers?" enquired Dr Loring.

Bob shook his head and said slowly and emphatically, "No question about that. Neither of them ever got fired from a job!"

Dr Loring rocked quietly for a moment before saying in a carefully neutral tone, "It's almost as if you just got a 'B' on your report card, and you're afraid of your father's disapproval. You didn't quite get that 'A' he expected from you. Once again, you failed to keep up with John and Tom, and as a result you're feeling thoroughly ashamed and guilt-ridden."

Bob's tension mounted as he pondered the doctor's words for several moments. He looked up at the psychologist and replied in a very strained voice. "Let me tell you, Dr Loring, I do feel exactly the same as I did when I thought I had disappointed my father...only this is worse. I didn't get a 'B'. I failed the course!" Bob covered his face with his hands.

The silence in the room was heavy.

After a time, Dr Loring began to talk, softly and patiently, as if explaining a very important point to a child. "In times of stress, we all regress to feelings we had in earlier times. The traumas of the past suddenly grab hold of us. We have a difficult time staying entirely in the present. We find we can't seem to sort out what's happening right now from what happened to us years ago. We revert to the habits of feeling and thinking we formed back then, maybe even as children. Right now, Bob, you're feeling a replay of the guilt and shame you felt so often, when you struggled to please your father."

Bob looked up at Dr Loring. "Only this time, I really did fall flat on my face. This isn't just a matter of a not-so-perfect grade on a report card. This time it's serious; it's a major screw up! I'm sure Dad wouldn't be at all pleased with me right now."

Dr Loring nodded. "This is what we call a visit from your unconscious, Bob. All your old feelings and memories are stored there, in the unconscious, and they come to visit you when you least expect them." He smiled at Bob. "You can think of them as unwelcome guests who drop in unannounced."

Bob gave a half-hearted grin in response to the psychologist's little joke. Then the tension returned to his face. "What can I do about these feelings?"

"You have to realise that a lot of time has passed," replied Dr Loring. "You don't need to please your father any more. You don't even have to compete with your brothers. You've grown up."

Bob took a deep breath. "Sometimes it's hard to feel that way," he muttered.

"I guess if your job hadn't become the biggest part of your identity, you might have landed on your feet," commented Dr Loring. "In other words, when you thought of yourself, Bob, you saw yourself as Mr National Sales Director, not as the many-faceted person you really are. That's why when you lost your job, in a sense you lost your very self." Dr Loring paused and let his words sink in. "You know, everyone reacts differently to what appears to be the same stressor. Some get over the impact of this kind of thing much faster than others, and a person's recovery rate is based on one thing."

"What's that?" inquired Bob.

Dr Loring leaned back in his chair and tented his fingers together. "In our House of Seven Cs, we have the four walls: *communication, confrontation, change* and *choice*. And we know that the roof of the house is *control*. The soil in which the house is rooted is *courage*."

Dr Loring paused for emphasis. "But the whole house is built on a foundation. Because the foundation supports the entire structure, it has to be firm and strong. Without a firm foundation, there can be no stability to the house. Bob, the foundation of our emotional house is *confidence,* and another word for confidence is self-esteem. Just like the foundation of any structure, the foundation of this house has to be sturdy enough so that it does not crack under stress. That means we need firm and unwavering confidence. It's our self-esteem that helps us believe in ourselves, no matter what the circumstances. And when we're looking at our emotional house, we need to consider the foundation of *confidence*. It's as important and basic as the soil, which, you remember, is *courage*."

Dr Loring rocked for a moment before he continued. Bob had the impression he was being given some time to assimilate what had been said before the psychologist continued.

"You see, Bob," Dr Loring went on, "the foundation of your emotional house is something you don't altogether choose. It grows out of your past, your history, your childhood. As a result of your early experience, it can be either rock-solid or weak. Confidence in *yourself* is the very foundation of your being. Without solid and positive feelings about *who you are*, you can never have firm belief in yourself or in anything else for that matter. And it's that firmness of belief in yourself, that rock-solid foundation of *confidence*, which allows the rest of the house to stand. *Confidence* and *courage* are the basis of your emotional house."

Bob thought about that for a minute. "Wait a minute, though," he said, "if we don't *choose* to have confidence, then how can we change it?"

The psychologist nodded approvingly. "Right," he said. "You don't choose to have self-esteem. But you *can* choose to recognise your own strengths and accomplishments – not in relation to anybody else's accomplishments, and not in order to win someone else's approval, but only in relation to what you want for yourself. You can choose to compete with yourself, to strive for your own improvement, instead of stacking yourself up against what somebody else is doing or has done. That's a losing game. By choosing to build, or rebuild, your confidence, you change the way you look at yourself. You begin to take charge of how you see yourself. You decide not to look at yourself through your brothers' eyes, or your father's eyes, but through your own. And to do this, you must step back and think about who you really are. In that way you build a good foundation, so your House of Seven Cs can stand firm."

"You mean I have to discard all those earlier feelings and memories because they may be destroying my self-confidence?" Bob asked. Before Dr Loring could answer, Bob continued, "But how can I do that? How can I forget what's already happened? And how can I forget how I felt about all those events?"

"You don't discard them," Dr Loring said. "What you do is try to see them differently. Try to understand the motivations of your parents and your brothers. Try to look back, from your present vantage point as an adult, to see yourself as a little boy growing up in that household. Try to see yourself through *their* eyes, and see your family from your present vantage point. If you do this, you'll begin to see your parents as just plain human beings, with weaknesses as well as strengths. Begin to see them as ordinary people, not the all-powerful figures of authority who knew everything and never made mistakes. Begin to understand their motivations, and you can begin to forgive them and love them in spite of their flaws."

Dr Loring lowered his voice and continued speaking gently and slowly. "If you do this, you will be able to see yourself differently – as a man capable in your own right, independent and grown up. Then you will relieve the pressure that's been building inside."

"I guess what you're saying," said Bob thoughtfully, "is that it's time I grew up to recognize who I *really* am. What I have done, what I am truly capable of. I don't have to keep comparing myself to my brothers." Bob paused, then said ruefully, "I guess you're asking me to take inventory."

"Exactly," Dr Loring said.

Suddenly, Bob looked frightened. "But, Dr Loring, 'who I am' is, or rather *was*, my *job*. Without my job, I don't know who I am!"

"Is that what you really think, Bob?"

"Absolutely," Bob said, as he shifted uneasily in his chair. "What am I now? What do I do? Nothing! I do nothing at all. And that's exactly how I feel – like nothing!"

The psychologist leaned forward. "One of the greatest problems most men have is that they identify too closely with their job. They can't tell where the job ends and where *they* begin. They don't really see themselves as people, just as whatever their job title calls them. This is true for some women, too, but to a lesser extent. In general, it seems to be a bigger problem for men."

"Why is that?" wondered Bob.

"Well," Dr Loring suggested, "women usually fill many roles at the same time. Even when they're out in the work world, very often they continue to take care of their homes, raise their children, keep in touch with their friends, and, perhaps, look after ageing parents. And women are used to reaching out to others for emotional support. They're not afraid about looking weak. In other words, they are *more* than their jobs. But men aren't inclined to reach out, or even to admit to anyone that they *need* emotional support. They tend to want to put all their eggs in one basket – and that's their work basket."

Bob nodded in agreement. "Okay, that makes sense. So I guess I'm one of those guys who really was one-sided. What do I do now to get rid of this feeling that without my job I'm nobody?"

"Well, the first step is one you've already taken," Dr Loring said in a reassuring tone. "The first step is to begin to take a really honest look at yourself. Ask yourself these questions: What have you accomplished in your lifetime? What did you contribute to your company when you were working there? Why did your wife marry you? Why do your children love you? Why did your father continually goad you to do better and better? It all boils down to one question, Bob: *who are you, beyond your job title?*"

Bob was silent for a few moments. "That's going to take a lot of thinking," he said quietly. "I don't have all those answers yet."

"That's what you're here for. If you can find the answers to those questions, Bob, you'll begin to understand who you really are. That's when you'll finally begin to achieve some balance in your life. You won't be driven by someone else's needs or desires. Just think, Bob, you'll finally get off the merry-go-round."

Bob looked at the psychologist curiously. "Why do you see me on a merry-go-round?" he asked.

"Isn't that a good metaphor for your life up to now?" Dr Loring asked. "Going round and round, up and down, and riding to someone else's music. Doesn't it sound familiar?"

"That's me, all right," Bob said.

Dr Loring shook his head. "That *was* you. You don't see yourself as having changed at all. You imagine that you're still fighting old childhood battles – battles you never really had a chance of winning because the cards were stacked against you." He paused and rocked back in his chair, waiting for Bob's response.

It was a few minutes in coming. Finally, Bob said tentatively, "So maybe it's time for me to leave the battlefield?"

"In a word, yes," Dr Loring said emphatically. "How do you feel about that?"

"Relieved, I guess," Bob admitted. "Maybe I don't have to ride the merry-go-round any longer. That feels good. I guess I'd have to say I feel somewhat at peace, too."

Dr Loring rose from his rocking chair and extended his hand to Bob. As the two men shook hands, the psychologist said, "Maybe now you can start getting at some of that shame and guilt you feel about losing your job. You know, we've just started examining the foundation of your house, Bob, and it seems to be a lot sturdier than you ever realised. Now, go home and think about all this and let's continue on this same path when I see you next week. How does that sound?"

Bob nodded his head. "It sounds as if I have a lot to think about."

It would not be an easy task, nor a rapid journey. Over the course of the next three weeks, Bob and Dr Loring unearthed more and more of Bob's past history. They talked about Bob's college years and about his interactions with his various siblings, his meeting Annie and how their relationship had broadened and deepened into marriage, his children and their childhood, and friendships he had developed through the years.

During this process, Bob began to perceive himself as a whole human being – more than a son and brother, more than a father and husband, and more than a job title. With Dr Loring's help, he began to put into perspective the different facets of his personality. He was surprised to discover that he had been inclined to overlook many of these parts of himself. He began to understand that he was more than a National Director of Sales. As his perception of himself widened, Bob began to feel like a whole person again, richer in personal truth than he had ever been before.

The days became a little longer. Spring seemed to be right around the corner and the air was a little softer. One day, Bob found himself thinking that maybe this spring he would be able to see and smell the flowers for the first time in years.

## *As we leave the site for the day, let's take notes*

1. Draw your lifeline by listing all the important events in your life – positive and negative – and the years in which they occurred.

2. Write down how you handled each of these events. What was the impact on your life of the negative ones? The positive ones?

3. How did you overcome the negative events? What did you do to lessen their impact?

4. What can you take from your past that will help firm up the foundation of your emotional house?

5. What have you accomplished in your lifetime – in all the spheres of your life?

6. What did you contribute to the companies you have worked for?

7. List the qualities you have now that will help you restore your self-confidence.

SITE VISIT 5

## *Your Choice – Letting Go*

AS THE WEEKS PASSED, BOB was beginning to see Dr Loring as an old and trusted friend. He felt quite comfortable during their sessions together. In their conversations, he found it less and less difficult to express his feelings about people and events, whether they were recent or far back in his past. It was toward the end of May that Bob realised that his feelings of anxiety had also lessened outside the sessions.

"How are you feeling these days, Bob?" Dr Loring asked. Both men had removed their jackets and were enjoying the pleasant breeze that drifted through the office window.

Bob leaned back in his chair and stretched his legs out in front of him. "I'd say things are a lot better. I'm definitely less anxious. But I don't think I'm out of the woods yet, Dr Loring."

"What do you mean by that?"

"Well," Bob continued, "I guess I'm still kind of preoccupied a lot of the time. Annie says she has to say things twice before I hear her. While my sleep is better than it was, it's still not great." A few moments passed as Bob thought about what he was feeling and searched for the right words. Then he looked up. "You know, as a matter of fact, I still don't really feel as though my job is gone. Every time I drive by Marter, I find myself starting to tense up. The other day I caught myself saying right out loud, 'Hey, this is MY company! How come I'm not there any more? What am I doing driving by like a stranger?' I get very angry at the injustice of it all. I still think I *ought* to be working there."

"Sounds as if you still feel like a victim," observed Dr Loring in a non-committal tone.

"Exactly," Bob agreed. "I *am* a victim! How long does this go on? When is that feeling going to go away?"

"When you decide it's time to let go," said the psychologist.

Bob looked surprised. "You mean I have a choice?" he asked,

Dr Loring nodded. "That's exactly what I mean," he replied. "and, as you already know, *choice* is the third wall of the emotional house you're rebuilding."

"I don't get it," Bob said in frustration. "What choice do I have when what I want is to go back to my old company and resume my old job? I can't just walk in there and sit down at my desk!"

"You do have a choice, though," Dr Loring insisted. "You can choose to accept or reject reality. The reality is that you cannot go back to the Marter Corporation. You cannot go back to your old job. You can accept that, or you can refuse to accept it. That's your choice."

"Boy, that's a hard one to swallow," muttered Bob.

Dr Loring shrugged. "If you're going to move on, you have to accept that you were dismissed from Marter. It's real. It happened. You can't change it. Accepting that reality is the only way you'll have a choice in how you handle the situation."

There was a note of self-pity in Bob's voice as he said, "Yeah, I guess – but it's tough feeling like a victim all the time."

"Well," the psychologist answered, "that's the point. By making that particular choice – continuing to see yourself as a victim, by continuing to feel sorry for yourself – you give your old company extraordinary power over you. You give Marter the power to bind you to old memories and manage your feelings."

"Wait a minute," Bob said, leaning forward in his chair, "are you saying I have a choice in how I *feel*? Do you mean I could choose to feel different?"

"That's right," Dr Loring said, nodding emphatically. "If you want to stop feeling like a victim, you have to make a conscious choice to say goodbye to your old company. It's like saying goodbye to an old friend. It may hurt, but it must be done. And by going out and finding new friends, you miss your old friend less and less."

Bob swallowed. "It's hard to throw away everything as if it never mattered," he said defensively.

Dr Loring held up a hand. "Wait a minute – I didn't say you have to throw away everything. I said you have to say *goodbye*. That's very different. There are ways to say goodbye. It's a lot like a mourning period, when someone close to you has died. You feel sad, lonely, bereft…and, hopefully, you share those feelings with someone you trust. You'll always miss the person who's gone, but by *expressing* the feelings that the death has brought out in you, you're learning to say goodbye. That's the only way you will be able to get on with your life, instead of being stuck in the rut of something that's past."

"Well, how do I get on with my life right now? I guess you're saying I'm still stuck at Marter."

"I think, Bob, in order to move on, you first have to say goodbye to the old life. You haven't really let go of it, you know. And to do that, you're going to need to step back a little and take a long, hard look at that old life."

"Oh, I think about it a lot, believe me. In fact, the truth is I think about it all the time!"

Dr Loring tapped his pencil on his pad. "I want you to think about your old job, your old company, in a *purposeful* way. I don't want it sneaking into your thoughts just any old time. I'd like you to *choose* when you're going to think about Marter. In order to do that, I want you to get some index cards. Then, choose an hour each day in which you plan to do nothing but think about your old company. Next, you're to take those cards and close yourself off from everyone and everything during that hour. Find a nice quiet place where no one will disturb you. Unplug the telephone, if you have to. Then, on each card, I want you to write a memory of Marter. These can be pleasant memories as well as unpleasant ones."

Dr Loring paused for emphasis then continued. "If you find that you're still thinking about the company when the hour is over, give yourself more time. That's your *choice*. You're going to be in *control* of when to mourn and when not to mourn. During your chosen time, give yourself permission to feel as miserable as you need to feel. Then you can control your feelings of misery at other times. When you're finished with your Marter Hour each day, sort the cards into two piles: *pleasant* and *unpleasant* memories. I'd like you to bring those cards to our next session."

Bob turned the doctor's instructions over and over in his mind. "You're saying I can *choose* when to think of my former company?" he asked. "And by choosing a particular time of day to concentrate on my old memories, I'm going to be more in charge of myself. Have I got that straight, Dr Loring?"

The psychologist nodded. "Exactly, Bob. By making this choice, you will exert some control over your feelings. Remember, *control* is the roof of the emotional house. You've probably noticed too, how each of the seven Cs is connected with the others…just like the walls of a house. It's very difficult to talk about one 'C' without connecting to another 'C'. The house can't stand unless every wall is in its proper place and connected to the next one."

"I can see how each 'C' is not alone," Bob said, "and every time you talk about one 'C', you usually bring in another one as well."

"That's right," Dr Loring said, "and now we're back to *confrontation* and *communication*. In order to say goodbye effectively, Bob, you're going to have to confront the fact that you are no longer a part of the Marter Corporation and communicate that in a way that will help you take control of the situation. So, every time you drive by your old company, I want you to say aloud, 'Goodbye, Marter Corporation. I miss you, but I'm moving on.'"

Bob looked astonished. "You must be joking," he said. "That sounds ridiculous, talking to myself in the car!"

"No, I'm dead serious," insisted Dr Loring. "This is a choice you can make. Say it every time: 'Goodbye, Marter Corporation. I miss you, but I'm moving on.' By doing this, *you* are making the choice of being proactive, rather than reactive. You're choosing not to be a victim. You're making a choice on that crossroads of crisis. You're choosing to venture out on the path of opportunity, instead of staying on the path of danger. *You* are taking control of the situation. Once you take control, you're no longer being kicked around by outside, or inside, forces. Bob, if you believe it's in your best interest to take control of your life, you'll make the choice of saying goodbye to Marter."

Bob pondered what the psychologist had said. "Are you saying," he asked slowly, "that by feeling miserable I am making a choice that is not in my best interest?"

"I'm saying that it's understandable that you still feel down," replied Dr Loring, "but I want you to start confining that feeling to one particular time of day. During the time you select, I want you to focus those feelings in a *constructive* way. Remember, Bob, you're working on constructing your emotional house so that it will be able to withstand stress. I don't want you to deny those feelings of grief and loss and anger," he went on. "I don't want you to pretend those feelings don't exist. If you keep them all locked up inside you, before long they'll be spilling over into every part of your life, and that would hardly be in your best interest." Bob nodded in agreement as Dr Loring spoke.

"By focusing those feelings," the doctor continued, "by forcing yourself to face the situation in an appropriate way, by taking control of your own feelings, you will begin to relieve the pressure inside you. You will face reality…and then you'll be able to get on with your life."

"That does make a lot of sense," Bob said. "Maybe it's not so crazy to say my farewells to Marter out loud. And writing down my memories of the company on cards…well, it's as good a way as any, I guess, to start saying goodbye."

Dr Loring smiled. "Right. And remember, Bob, you cannot say hello to something new, to whatever is around the next corner in your life, until you've finished saying goodbye to what's past. Do those two exercises and next week I'll be very interested to hear what you have to say about them."

On his way home from the psychologist's office, Bob made a special point of driving past the Marter Corporation. It didn't feel as strange as he had expected when he said firmly, "Goodbye, Marter Corporation. I miss you, but I'm moving on."

He even gave a jaunty little wave to the Marter building as he turned the corner. Looking in the rear-view mirror, Bob watched his old company recede into the distance and realised that that was what was going to happen to his memories of Marter – particularly the bad ones. They were going to recede into the distance. A lopsided grin covered Bob's face. Maybe this was going to work after all.

## *As we leave the site for the day, let's take notes*

1. What choices have you made to leave the danger zone?

2. Write down how you choose to take advantage of each day.

3. Write down what you choose to eat each day...when you choose to exercise...when you choose to call your friends.

4. Do you choose to remain positive in your thinking no matter what the difficulties? If not, why not?

5. When you get a rejection in your job search, how do you choose to respond to that?

6. Do the exercise Dr Loring has prescribed for Bob. Get some index cards, find a quiet place, and choose the time of day for your reflection. Confront your pleasant and unpleasant memories and communicate them by writing them on the index cards. Please follow Dr Loring's instructions exactly.

Site Visit 6

## *Moving On*

EACH DAY DURING THE NEXT WEEK, Bob scheduled one hour to sit by himself in his study without interruption. On the first day, he felt a bit awkward as he shut himself off from his immediate world and concentrated on the pile of index cards that sat on the desk in front of him. As he began to concentrate on the beginning of his career at Marter and let his memories take over, he began to get into the process. Before he knew it, he was beginning to classify his memories as either 'good' or 'bad.' When he began to tire, Bob looked at the clock and was amazed to find that he had been at this exercise for almost two hours. He put each pile of cards into envelopes, marked them 'good' and 'bad,' and went to join his family. He was surprised at how fatigued he was. He felt as if he had run a marathon.

On the second day, Bob was eager to continue the process of 'the cards'. At first, he found he had more good memories than bad. But as he began to search deep inside himself, he soon realised that many of his negative feelings were coming from the times he missed with his family. Bob became aware that by putting the company first, he had missed irreplaceable moments in the lives of his children...their growing-up years. He also felt very guilty about not being there for Annie when she ran into difficulty with one of the children, or when she needed him for herself. He didn't miss everything, but he certainly wasn't around many times when his presence would have been of great benefit.

As his thoughts wandered back over his life, Bob realised how lucky he was that his marriage was still intact. Its endurance certainly wasn't due to anything he had done. Because Annie didn't complain and shared in his vision, she had accepted doing double-duty as part of their contract together. Now that he looked back, he wondered – if she had complained, would he have changed? Knowing himself and his single-minded effort to earn the title 'company man,' Bob recognised that he never would have listened. If anything, his marriage would probably have failed. Because Annie was strong and resolute as virtually a single parent (yes, he sighed, that was really how she functioned all those years), Bob had been able to follow his dream. When he finally finished his index cards for that day, two hours after he had begun, Bob felt enormous guilt about how he had treated his family, especially since his dream had turned into a nightmare. He cleared his desk and decided to go for a long walk by himself in order to clear his mind and heart.

By the third day, Bob was putting his life more into perspective. He thought more about his values and less about good and bad memories. He was surprised to find that after the hour had elapsed, the piles of cards hadn't really grown much from the day before. He felt stronger and more at ease. At the end of his time alone, Bob looked forward to joining his family to find out how their day was going.

His fourth session began slowly but picked up energy as he began to sort out the incidents of his career at Marter. At the end of the hour, Bob noticed how much lighter he felt. It was as if he had emptied his mind of what was no longer needed so that other things could enter. He was making room for his life to continue.

By the fifth day, Bob found he really didn't have much to write about. After 45 minutes of thinking about the Marter Corporation, and coming up with memories he'd already recorded, he decided to call it a day. He was looking forward to his next visit with Dr Loring.

– o –

As he settled into his chair in Dr Loring's office, Bob couldn't help grinning. Opening his attaché case, he took out two sizeable packets of index cards. A wide red elastic band encircled the larger packet, while the smaller packet bore a blue band.

"Well, how did you do with your assignment, Bob?" Dr Loring inquired.

"Well, actually, I think I did amazingly well. The first day I really needed more than an hour. I kept thinking of more and more memories I wanted to write down, so I just kept going. At the end of that time I felt really drained. I couldn't have thought about the company any more even if I'd wanted to."

Dr Loring's smile encouraged Bob. "How did it go during the rest of the week?" he asked. "Did you find you needed more than an hour every day?"

"Not after the second day," Bob replied. "By the third day, one hour was just about right. And the fourth day I really didn't even need the whole hour. In fact, yesterday, I 'dredged' for only half an hour, and that was all I could manage."

"And were you able to concentrate on other things during the day?" Dr Loring asked.

"Not at first," Bob said, "but when I got to the third day, I felt different. And that surprised me. I really didn't find myself drifting off into thoughts of my old company at all. After I finished the exercise, I actually wrote up my resumé and began to telephone some people I know to tell them I'm looking for a job."

"Well, that's a big step forward," Dr Loring said. "You know, Bob, you seem different today. Even the way you're telling me this story is matter-of-fact and positive. It doesn't sound as though there's too much shame and guilt left. Am I right?"

"Yeah, I guess you're right," Bob agreed. Then he thought for a minute and said slowly, "I just feel angry and hurt. Writing down all those memories made me see a number of things I missed before."

"Can you give me some examples?" asked the psychologist.

"Well, I have very pleasant memories of my quick climb up the ladder," said Bob. "The company believed in me then. They made a big investment in me, and I felt valued and worthwhile. But then, while I was writing on those cards, I began to see how the company started to change. Their objectives and mine weren't the same any more. I guess I just failed to read the signals." Even as Bob described the way his goals had begun to differ from those of the Marter Corporation, his voice remained strong and sure. The note of self-pity and borderline desperation that had been evident for so many weeks had disappeared.

"I thought I could ride it out," Bob continued. "I figured that if I just gave a little more of myself, of my time and my energy, things would work out for the best. What has really struck me, though, was how naive I was to think my sacrifice would be appreciated."

"Appreciated by whom?" asked Dr Loring.

"By the company, of course. Certainly not by Annie and the kids. They sacrificed as much as I did. Annie functioned as a single parent and my kids felt that they didn't have a father, all because I thought that what I did for the company would eventually pay off for me and my family. And I really resent the fact that the company forgot about everything I did for them. So what I did was to mark with a red pencil those unpleasant memories that infuriated me the most."

"Good idea," the psychologist nodded. "So let's talk about some of those memories you marked with red."

Bob launched into a discussion of various incidents at the

Marter Corporation. He was surprised at how angry he could feel by just talking about them, but by doing so he began to put them into their proper perspective. For the most part, Dr Loring just sat and listened, but every so often he asked a question that gave Bob a fresh way to look at the experience. By the end of the hour, Bob had just begun to get started and found it difficult to put it all away. He looked forward to his next appointment.

When Bob saw Dr Loring again, he was still eager to recount his unpleasant times at the Marter Corporation. Dr Loring encouraged Bob to continue and examine the details of his career.

By the middle of the hour, when Bob paused for a bit, Dr Loring remarked, "I notice you don't seem so angry as you were a few days ago."

"Oh, I'm still angry," Bob said, "but I don't feel so miserable. The more I talk about it, the more I'm beginning to think they may have done my family and me a favour."

Dr Loring looked up alertly. "In what way?"

"Well, as I did this exercise," Bob began rather slowly, "I've had a lot of time to think. If I had stayed at Marter, I never would have begun to look at my life and what it was all about. Besides bringing in a lot of money, I don't think I would have awakened to my other responsibilities as a husband and father. Would anyone ever have been able to tell me that I was cheating my family and myself by climbing the corporate ladder at Marter? I doubt it. If they did, I would have claimed that they just didn't understand, that I was doing it all for my family. So how could I have been cheating my family? All this doesn't mean I'm glad I lost my job. I just mean maybe I can get things right this time, so I can have both worlds. Do you know what I mean?"

Dr Loring nodded. "I think you have to ask yourself what you can take with you to your new job that will stand you in good stead in the future. Don't throw your ambition away. Just learn to temper it, so that you can be a good husband and father and still be successful in your work. Let's write a job description of what you mean by 'good husband and father' before you think about your goals for the future."

Bob was quiet for a while. For the first time in his life, he was going to have to define himself – not as part of a company – but as part of a family. It was no easy task. Finally, Bob said slowly and deliberately, "A good husband and father are really one and the same. He puts his family before everything. They are his number one priority."

"That's quite a statement, Bob. How do you feel saying that?"

"I have a lot of guilt about how I performed those jobs during most of my married life," Bob answered quietly. "When I think of all the years I didn't do that, I feel a lot of regret. I know I wasn't what you would call a good father or good husband. I thought just being able to give my family more and more material things made me feel I was doing things right. I also thought success in the company would make Annie proud of me. I guess I let my own ambition blot out what was really going on."

Bob looked drained as he sat back to collect his thoughts. After a while, Dr Loring broke the silence. "That was then, Bob. How about now?"

"Now? Now I feel very different. Now that I have taken the time to step back and see what's really important, I also have a feeling of satisfaction. I think I'm finally able to live that job description," Bob responded. There was a certain amount of pride in his voice and in his bearing.

"You've got the whole ball of wax when you define it like that, Bob. You have really created your own mission statement…your own sense of purpose. If you can live that way, you'll know what to do about your goals for the future. You know, Bob," Dr Loring said, leaning forward in his rocking chair with a serious expression on his face, "I think you're ready now to let go of the past – the unpleasant past – the past that led you here. What do you think?"

Bob paused for a moment, then smiled at the psychologist. "I think you're right."

Dr Loring continued. "I want you to keep all the good memories, the index cards in the blue band. When the going gets rough, refer to them, learn from them. They'll help you repair any cracks in your foundation of confidence. But as for the cards with the red elastic, I want you to get rid of them as fast as possible. When you leave here today, I want you to go home and burn those cards in the fireplace. As they burn, say goodbye to them."

"Out loud?" Bob asked with a grin. He knew by now that the good doctor didn't see anything unusual in talking to inanimate objects.

"You bet," Dr Loring said. "Say goodbye to the cards, which are all your unhappy memories of the Marter Corporation." In his best instructional tone, Dr Loring went on to explain. "By burning those cards, you are performing a ritual. We go through many rituals in life – weddings and funerals, to name just two. They give meaning and significance to our lives. They also allow us to move forward. By going through this ritual of burning the cards, you are attending a funeral and saying your final goodbye to the unpleasant part of the Marter Corporation. In this way, you may find it easier to let go and to get rid of the anger you've felt, as well as those feelings of victimisation." Dr Loring tapped on his notepad for emphasis. "It's time for you to move on, Bob. Don't you think so?"

Bob nodded in agreement. "You're right," he said. "But don't think I'm not scared," he added hastily. "I still haven't got a job."

"There's nothing wrong with being scared," the psychologist said. "That's perfectly okay. What's not okay is keeping all that anger and bitterness locked up inside you. That's what robs you of your energy. You're going through some big changes, Bob, and all change brings fear and anxiety with it, even change for the better. You need your energy to take charge of this change in your life."

"Okay, I'll buy that." Bob wasn't about to dispute Dr Loring's assertion that change brings fear and anxiety – he'd been feeling those emotions on and off for months. "But how do I handle this business of not having a job? How do I get rid of the fear and anxiety you mentioned?"

Once again, in that familiar gesture that Bob was getting to know so well, Dr Loring tented his fingers under his chin. "I think you're about ready to put up the fourth wall of your emotional house, Bob – and that's *change*. As I was just saying, all change, good and bad, brings stress. Why do you suppose that is?"

Bob searched for a response, but the psychologist answered his own question. "It's because there's always a sense of loss involved with change – the loss of familiar things that tend to make us feel safe and secure. For example, do you remember when your first child was born?"

"Of course I do," Bob replied. "And yeah, you're right, I'd say that was big-time stress!"

"That's because you changed something in your familiar pattern of life," Dr Loring said. "You and Annie went from a family with two people to three. And when the next baby came, you went from a family with one child to a family with two children. Each of these changes, while happy and positive events, involved loss as well as gain. I'm sure you can think of some of the losses you experienced with those changes."

Bob grinned ruefully. "I sure can," he nodded. "The biggest loss, of course, was the time that Annie and I could spend together, doing whatever we felt like. And I remember feeling kind of jealous of the kids sometimes, because she spent so much time taking care of them and doing things for them. It seemed she did not have much time for just me any more. Not to mention the fact that money had to be spent for family necessities instead of vacations and special things that caught our eye. Oh yes, I can think of quite a few losses around that time."

"And each of those changes required you to shift gears, so to speak," Dr Loring noted. "It's that transition period, the time it takes to go from one state or condition to the new state or condition, that's so stressful. Once you've settled into the new condition, your stress level drops again."

"So is there some way to handle change so that it's not so stressful?" Bob wondered.

"Well," the psychologist began, rocking gently in his chair, "there are different ways of looking at change. One way of seeing change can make you feel very anxious and even fearful. If you look at it another way, you feel stimulated, excited, full of vitality and eagerness to meet a new challenge. You have to think of change as a crossroads, Bob. One path is known to you, and you feel safe walking it because you're familiar with every turn and every variance in the surface. The other path is foreign and strange; you can't see very far along it, and you don't know what lies ahead around the bend. The question is, how *adventurous* are you? And how *courageous*?" Dr Loring stopped for emphasis, allowing his words to sit a moment.

Finally, the psychologist continued, "Remember that the earth supporting your house is *courage,* and that the earth needs to be firm and strong in order to allow you to welcome change as a challenge that you're capable of meeting."

"To tell you the truth, Dr Loring, I look at this change with a lot of fear," Bob admitted. "I don't see it as a challenge. Too much depends on it, and I don't know if I'm up to it. Frankly, I'm scared to death. Is there anything I can do to make it easier?"

Dr Loring nodded. "Bob, here's where we go back to another wall of your house, one you've already built: *choice*. You have to choose how you're going to view this change. If you see change as unsettling, as something that's disturbing to your level of comfort, safety, and security, then you're going to feel an inordinate amount of fear, and what some people call 'bad stress'. On the other hand, if you choose to look at change as a challenge – as a new opportunity for growth, revitalisation, and wider horizons – then you will welcome change as a friend, instead of avoiding it as an enemy. And, of course, there is the foundation of your emotional house. The more you can call forth your successes in life, the greater your *confidence* will be in yourself as you go through change."

Bob shifted uncomfortably in his chair. "Sounds easier said than done," he muttered.

"I didn't say it was easy," said the psychologist. "I only mean that the more quickly you can stop being afraid, then the more quickly you'll move out of the danger zone and into the zone of opportunity. And when you can do that, your stress level will diminish faster."

"Okay, then, how do I do it? Tell me how to stop being afraid so that I can see this whole business as an opportunity." Bob did not bother to hide his belligerence as he challenged the doctor for an answer.

"You've already started," Dr Loring said in a reassuring tone. "By putting down on those index cards all your pleasant and unpleasant memories of Marter, you have started the process of change. You keep the cards in the packet with the blue band. That way you take all the pleasant memories with you. The investment the company made in you and that you made in the company is yours to keep and use for your growth. If Marter chose not to take full advantage of their investment, then that's their loss. But it's to your benefit to realise that you still have those strengths that they saw and nurtured in you. That's how you rebuild the foundation of your emotional house." Bob looked up in surprise. He had never looked at his job loss as Marter's loss. "Now what you need to do," Dr Loring went on, "is to *choose* to place those strengths elsewhere and begin the process of growth all over again."

Bob took a moment to think before he said, "It sounds like there's a long road ahead."

"Maybe it's long," the psychologist concurred, "but it can also be exciting. It all depends upon how you choose to perceive it. In order to turn this situation around, Bob, you have to make a conscious choice to see it in a different way. You have to explore the various facets of this change, make yourself aware of what it can bring into your life that will benefit you and your family. Can you think of some ways in which you could view the loss of your job as a gain? Is there anything here that could be an opportunity rather than a disaster? I'd like you to take time and think about that now."

Bob reflected for nearly a minute before he spoke. "I can tell you that Annie and I are much closer now than we were before. I'm finding it easier to tell her how I'm feeling without expecting the sky to fall. And I'm definitely spending more time to be with the kids. In fact, I saw my son Eric play football the other night. I hadn't been able to do that for a long time. I was always either travelling or working late. Now my daughter sits with me each evening to tell me about her day, and that's something that was unheard of when I was working."

"That's a great example of what we were talking about before – how your roles of husband and father are being enhanced. It seems as if you're feeling more fulfilled in your personal life."

"I would say so," Bob said, "although actually I never thought much about that before."

Dr Loring made a brief note on his pad and asked, "Are there any advantages of this loss to you and your family from a professional standpoint?"

"Well, my wife and I have talked a lot about the possibilities," Bob acknowledged. "Annie says she's willing to move anywhere we can find a good opportunity. In fact, she said she's always wanted to have the experience of living somewhere else. She grew up just a few miles from here, and she thinks it would be exciting to try living in another part of the country. Although Alicia said at the beginning of all this that she'd never leave her high school, I think she's coming around. With Eric going off to college next year, Alicia has said how lucky she thinks he is to have the chance to try something new. So, I think, as a family, we're going to be able to work out the kinks as we never were able to before."

Bob went on quite animatedly. "Annie also suggested I try to find a place with a smaller company, one that wouldn't require me to be involved in all the international travel that Marter did. She doesn't feel we really need all the money we thought we did. This house is bigger than we need, now that both kids will be ready to move out into their own lives – Eric next year and Alicia in three. We've gone over our finances pretty closely and we know we'll be okay as long as we're careful. In fact, we all sit down now, as a family, and go over the budget. Everyone is contributing in cutting down expenses. The kids are getting summer jobs and saving for college, and they both plan to apply for scholarships."

Bob stretched his arms over his head and grinned at the psychologist. It had been a long, deep, and rewarding session. "You know, when I had a job I never would have allowed this to happen," he continued. "I would have felt demeaned because it was my place to bring in the money. So, is this an opportunity? If you look at all those changes in my life – my family telling me it's not just my responsibility to run a house but *theirs* too, how much closer I feel to all of them, and how much I feel they love me and understand what I'm going through – then, yeah, you could definitely say we've all gained something we never had before I lost my job."

"Good for you, Bob," Dr Loring said. "By doing this kind of planning, you're taking the first step toward taking control of the situation, instead of letting the situation control you."

"I do feel I'm on top of things more these days," Bob said. "It's been quite a while since I had that feeling. Just sitting here and listening to myself talk about this makes me see how much better it all is. In fact, I can't believe I feel this way, considering what happened."

The psychologist stood up. "Funny you should mention being on top of things, because next week, we'll complete that emotional house you've been rebuilding. You're ready to put the roof on the house now – and the roof, you recall, is *control*. But you have plenty to think about this week. Let's save that for our next session. And don't forget to burn that pack of index cards when you get home."

"Right," Bob said, replacing the cards in his attaché case. "I have quite a few goodbyes to say tonight, haven't I! Thanks, Dr Loring, I'll see you next week."

## *As we leave the site for the day, let's take notes*

❶ Just as Bob did the exercise with the index cards, you are to follow Dr Loring's advice and do exactly the same thing: Get some index cards, choose a time of day and shut yourself off from everything people, telephones, interruptions of any kind. Plan to spend an hour each day 'dredging up' old memories of your last job before your 'firing'. Decide whether they are good or bad memories and put them in the appropriate piles.

❷ Find someone to talk to about these memories and go over your list, bad ones first.

❸ After you have 'cleansed' yourself of the bad memories, burn the cards, just as Dr Loring suggested to Bob.

❹ Keep the good memories and re-read them once a week while you feel the need for support.

❺ As you reflect on your career and family life, if you could change one thing, what would it be?

❻ Define your values in life now that you have lost your job. Do you have new goals?

❼ How have you benefited from this loss? Write down the positive changes that have taken place in your life.

❽ Are you able to view your job loss as an opportunity rather than as a disaster?

Site Visit 7

## *Taking Control*

As THE WEEKS WENT BY, Bob gradually gained insight into his situation, and more importantly, into himself. He found himself taking charge of more areas of his life, and discovered that when he felt powerless, he generally had very little control of the situation. During those times, when he felt he lacked authority or influence, he felt his stress level begin to rise, but he was able step back and realise there were some things that were simply out of his control, things he could do nothing about. He concluded that assuming control of something, almost anything, might help diminish the stress.

"Good morning, Bob," Dr Loring began. "How are things going?"

"Well, I started my swimming again," Bob said. "For a while I just couldn't seem to muster up the interest or the desire to bother going to the gym. But this week, I figured it was time to do something positive just because I wanted to."

"That's great," Dr Loring said. "It sounds as if you're getting back in control of your life."

Bob nodded. "Yeah, I think so. At least I can decide whether or not I'm going to swim. It's been a long time since I've felt I had the time to swim regularly. I guess that's another advantage of being out of my former company."

"I notice you said *former* company," the psychologist observed. "That word tells me that you're learning to put the past behind you. Is that true?"

"Well," Bob said, "I did as you suggested. Every time I drove by Marter, I simply said goodbye to it, right out loud. At first, I felt kind of ridiculous doing that – talking out loud to myself in the car, I mean. But suddenly I started meaning it. I'd say, 'Goodbye, Marter Corporation. I miss you but I'm moving on' – and one day I realised I was moving on. And then when I went home and burned those bad memories of Marter, that was *really* weird. But, before I knew it, I really started feeling that I'm not guilty of doing anything wrong, and I'm free to do as I want, with no strings attached. It's strange how different it felt."

Dr Loring gave Bob a thumbs-up sign. "I knew you'd be a good builder, Bob," he said. "Now, let's see what you've built so far. You have definitely *confronted* the situation of your job loss and *communicated* with your family; but more significantly, you've confronted it within *yourself*. By learning how to say goodbye to the past, you're ready to meet the future."

"I certainly do feel a lot better," Bob acknowledged. "But if I said I wasn't still anxious about getting a new job, I'd be lying."

"That kind of anxiety is perfectly in order. When we get to the next part of this house you're building, I think even the stress that comes from anxiety about your next job will be lowered," the psychologist said. "You see, Bob, you've learned that there are things you can control. You've taken charge of your memories, of your time in mourning your loss, and now you've taken charge of your swimming. You are showing yourself again and again that you're capable of rising from the ashes."

Bob looked surprised. "You're right," he said slowly. "I never thought of it that way. I didn't understand that just choosing to swim and getting myself down to the pool was a major accomplishment. For a long time I felt so crushed that I thought I'd never be able to do anything again, and I mean anything." Bob paused, lowered his eyes, and then blurted out, "There were weeks there when I couldn't even make love to my wife!"

"Does that surprise you?" Dr Loring asked. "You'd just been hit right in your self-esteem. Your confidence in yourself had hit rock bottom. When you lose your confidence, particularly your confidence in yourself as a man, it affects every aspect of your performance as a male."

"You mean that happens to other guys in my situation?" Bob's relief was almost comical. "I thought I was a total failure, a nothing!"

"We talked about this sort of thing a few weeks ago, remember?" Dr Loring reminded him. "Men, in particular, identify so closely with their jobs that without one they have no idea who they are. Most men don't see themselves as anything but their job description. That's what drives them. It's their sense of self. Without it, they feel worthless. That's when they are in the danger zone and can't even begin to imagine the possibility of opportunity."

"I know what you mean," agreed Bob. "And one of those opportunities we talked about last time has been the chance to find that I can function as a good husband and father."

"By losing one part of yourself – and you had to become aware that it was just one part – you began to find other parts," Dr Loring said. "Actually, these parts you're just discovering are the most important ones. Your finding yourself as a husband and father will be with you long after any job is gone."

Bob stirred restlessly in his chair. "But, not to labour the point, Dr Loring, I'm still worried about getting a job. I have to provide for my family. Yes, I know my wife and kids are great in cutting expenses, but let's face it, it's still my job to be the chief breadwinner. It won't be long before we start in on our savings. I've got to get something lined up soon."

"Believe it or not, Bob, you first had to provide for yourself," insisted the psychologist. "If you have nothing but emptiness inside yourself, what can you do for anyone else? What goes in, comes out. It's as simple as that."

Bob repeated Dr Loring's words in his head. *What goes in, comes out.* When he spoke again, it was with greater understanding of himself. "Then I'm not being selfish by taking the time to swim and to spend more time with Annie and the kids."

"On the contrary, far from it. By taking that time for yourself and time with your family, you're rebuilding your House of Seven Cs. Remember *confidence* is the foundation on which the house is placed. The more successful you see yourself – in as many ways as possible – the greater your self-confidence. Right now, particularly, you need to feel you're achieving something, that you're doing something well. That's why taking charge of your exercise programme is important. Proving to yourself that you can be an attentive husband and caring father is of great importance. Without self-esteem or confidence in yourself, the house won't stand."

"That's all very well and good, doctor," Bob said in frustration, "but for my confidence in myself to be really firm, I need a job!"

"Yes, you do Bob. Granted." The psychologist leaned back in his rocking chair. "So let's go back for a bit to *change* and *control*. Remember that *control* is the roof of your house. To complete your reconstruction, you need to gain more control over your life than you feel you have now. And since change is what brought you here in the first place, let's see how you can use change so that *you* control the situation, not the other way around. The key to control is in your knowing where you want to go and then deciding what you need to do to get there."

"Oh, I know where I want to go, all right," Bob responded immediately.

"I wonder if you really do," replied Dr Loring in a carefully neutral tone. "Bob, I would like you to do another exercise before we see each other again next week. I want you to give some thought to your long-term goals; and then I want you to write down your goals for two years, five years and ten years from now. But I want you to write these goals in terms of your age. For example, since you're 48 now, where do you want to be when you're 50, 55 and 60? And when I ask you where you want to be, I mean in several areas. First, professionally: in what kind of job or position do you imagine yourself? Second, financially: how much money do you want to be earning, and how much security do you want to have amassed? And third, personally: where do you want to live? What kind of house do you want to live in? What do you have in mind for your children at that time?"

"Whew," Bob remarked. "Sounds like a tall order."

"It is a tall order," the psychologist agreed, "but it's the route to finding a new job. After you get all this down on paper, you can use it as a framework for figuring out three things: what kind of job you should be seeking; the kind of company you want to join in order to realise your financial, personal, and professional goals; and where this company needs to be located. For instance, do you see yourself in a small, growing company, or a large national or multinational corporation? You mentioned in a previous session that you and your wife have already begun to think about this. Your wife felt that a smaller company would be better for you, but I want more specific thinking about this. Do your own objectives match the objectives of the companies you are pursuing? This kind of knowledge about where you're going will motivate you toward a plan of action that will be much more direct and less haphazard than the typical job search."

Bob sat up straighter in his chair. He looked animated, even excited. "It sounds like this would be a great way to get on top of my worries about getting a job," he said. "This really gives me a strong sense of direction. It makes me feel as though there's something concrete I can do."

"Exactly," Dr Loring concurred. "Now you are beginning to take control of the process. You will also find you'll feel less panicky in terms of your present financial situation and your goals, if you know exactly how much time is needed to acquire this job. This kind of plan will keep you from jumping into the first job you're offered, just to allay your anxiety about being out of work. This will cap our project and put the roof on your house."

"Sounds good," Bob said enthusiastically. "Now, am I supposed to share this with Annie?"

"Absolutely," Dr Loring nodded. "The two of you need to do this together. In the final analysis, you alone will have to decide which job to take, but you need your wife's input in order to get to that point. Again, as you did during the first exercise, find a place where you'll be uninterrupted, and leave the answering machine on – don't take any calls," he suggested with a little smile. "Use index cards to record each goal. Each of you is to fill out your own cards separately, at first. Just write down what you think you want, without filtering any of it out, no matter how far-fetched it may seem. Then when you go over the cards together, you'll begin to see what compromises will have to be made between the two of you, and find what fits and what doesn't in your grand long-term scheme. At that point, you can begin sorting things out and deciding which actions to take first."

"This is going to take quite a bit of time," Bob said. "Annie and I had better set aside quite a few evenings to do this."

"Good idea," the psychologist said, "and, as I said before, be sure you'll be uninterrupted during that time. Now, there's one more facet to this exercise. I'd like you to write down after each of your stated goals a first *practical* step you must take *immediately* in order to accomplish each goal. Once you get to that stage, you'll really be in control because you will actually be doing something."

"Sounds great," Bob said. He rose from his chair and picked up his attaché case. "I'll go home and tell Annie about this right away."

As Dr Loring opened his office door, the two men shook hands. "Bob, you sound motivated and in charge," the doctor said, "happy thinking – and doing. Have a great week."

## *As we leave the site for the day, let's take notes*

**You are to do this exercise exactly as Dr Loring outlined it to Bob in this session. If you are married, be sure to do this exercise with your spouse.**

❶ What are your long-term goals?
- Break this down into two-year goals, five-year goals and ten-year goals.
- Write these down in terms of your age. Where do you want to be at _____ (put in age)?

❷ Be specific in terms of personal goals:
- Where do you want to live?
- What kind of house do you want?
- If you have children, what do you have in mind for them at that time?

❸ Be specific in terms of financial goals:
- How much money do you need to earn in order to fulfill your personal goals?
- How much money do you want as a reserve?
- What about a retirement plan: do you have one ongoing or do you have to begin one?

❹ Be specific in terms of your professional goals:
- What kind of job or position are you qualified for?
- Given your educational and experiential resources, what kind of job should you be seeking?
- Given your ambition, in what kind of company should you be working?
- Given your personal and financial goals, where should this company be located?
- Do your own goals match the goals of the companies you are pursuing?

❺ What can you do *now* in order to begin accomplishing one of your goals?

❻ Write down how you're constructing the roof of your house. Have you taken control of anything in your life? What?

Site Visit 8

## *From Danger To Opportunity*

BOB AND ANNIE SPENT MANY hours going over their life goals together. As a result, they found they were communicating as they never had before. They began to share their feelings and their thoughts with each other. Because feelings of trust between them grew day by day, they were able to confront issues in a way that allowed them to solve many of their disagreements. Not only were they involved in planning a new life together, they were growing as a couple, making increasingly effective efforts to move away from danger and toward opportunity. After much discussion, they decided to put together three goal sheets, labeled 'his', 'hers', and 'ours'.

Bob took the goal sheets with him to his next session. When Dr Loring asked how things had gone, Bob wasted no time in responding that he and Annie had worked long and hard to come up with some answers. He took out the three goal sheets so he could share them with the psychologist.

"For example," Bob said, "Annie and I disagree on a few of our goals. She feels that I shouldn't go near a multinational company. She's afraid of what my ambition would do to me in that kind of environment. I disagree, only because *all* companies today need to grow in order to stay alive. If I'm going to have a career of any kind and, let's face it, I'm only 48-years-old, I have to be with a growing company. It may not be a multinational now, but it well might become one if its products, marketing, and sales are any good. And that's really how I see my job in sales…to grow the company. So no matter where I am, I'm going to strive to improve the company's position."

"Sounds as if Annie may be afraid of your ambition," commented Dr Loring. "Would she be more comfortable if you ran a neighbourhood grocery?"

"We talked that one out. But even a neighbourhood grocery has to be innovative if it's going to stay alive. You're right though," Bob agreed. "She is afraid of my ambition and my need to be successful."

"Have you got any suggestions for helping her deal with that fear?" Dr Loring asked as he continued taking notes.

"Well, we talk about what we both want, and I try to reassure her that I've changed because of all that's happened and that things will be different from now on."

The psychologist thought for a moment, then said, "I think for you and Annie to lessen your anxiety about a new job, you have to be clear about what will be expected of you. Granted, you can only do that up to a point, but you can get a clue if you interview the company as well as letting them interview you. For example, you have to ask how the company views the family. Will they want you to sacrifice yourself to their bottom line? You have to talk with some of the employees. I think in this way you will focus in very quickly on the management style they value and see whether you will fit in. You and your wife both have to realise that you must compromise some of your requirements in order for you to get and keep a job. The climate today is a tough one, and if you want to be part of the current scene, you must be willing to compromise a bit. I didn't say give away your lives, but some form of moderation in your views may be necessary."

Bob and the doctor continued their conversation, weeding out some of the differences between Bob and Annie in order to come to a more balanced approach. The reality of the marketplace had to be confronted, as well as the goals of both husband and wife, individually and collectively.

After they finished discussing the goal sheets, Dr Loring said approvingly, "Well, Bob, it looks to me as if you have some sense of direction now, and a lot less anxiety. You've come a long way."

"It's true," Bob agreed. "Annie and I have begun to think about the kind of life we'd like to share together, and that puts a whole new light on this job-hunting project. It's strange that we never really took the time to talk this way before."

The psychologist smiled. "And I assume you like talking together."

Bob returned Dr Loring's smile. "No question about that. We're closer than we've ever been, even in the beginning. Somehow I don't feel I'm carrying that burden of responsibility that weighed so heavily on me. I always thought I had to do all the protecting, that it was my job as the husband and that she wasn't supposed to worry about finances or planning our lives or any of that. Now I know that it wasn't fair to Annie to leave her out of the major decisions. I see that we both need to share the burden together. And that's something I never really felt before."

"I guess your wife could say the same thing," remarked Dr Loring. "How do you think she feels about all this?"

"Until this happened, I never took the time to find out how she was feeling," admitted Bob. "But now...well, Annie said the other night that she felt we could get through any trouble at all as long as we stood together this way. And we're thrilled about the kids. They're growing because of this, too. They seem so much more mature to me, so...responsible. It's like talking to two adults. It just makes me feel great."

Dr Loring nodded. "You seem to have discovered a very important fact, Bob. Communication is a two-way street – there is *talking* and there is *listening*, and both of them have to be there for the communication to be effective. Sometimes I think communication is also *looking*. You finally took time out to look at your children, and when you did you decided to listen to them. That's when you discovered they're not the babies of yesterday. While you were busy providing for them, they decided to grow up."

There was a long pause as Bob digested the psychologist's words. "You know, Dr Loring," he said at last, "I've discovered something else, too. My work with you has been one hell of a learning experience. You've really shown me things that I never even dreamed about."

"Well, Bob, you took the mystery out of psychology by mustering up your courage to come and see me," Dr Loring said. "That was a big step, and you were able to take it. All the rest has come out of that first step."

Another long pause ensued. "It's funny," Bob said, "but every time I've come here I've had so much to talk about that I never thought 50 minutes would be enough. Often it wasn't, and we had to carry something over for another week."

"And now...?" prompted the psychologist.

"Well, today I just don't seem to have very much to talk about," Bob said, shrugging his shoulders.

The psychologist laid his pencil and his lined pad on the desk beside the rocking chair where he sat. He smiled at Bob, an open smile of respect and appreciation. "That means that we have reached the end of our journey together, Bob. You're a superb builder. You've worked very hard, and you've built a sound and sturdy emotional house. It's standing securely on the firm, strong foundation of your *confidence*, which is rooted in the healthy and nourishing soil of your *courage*."

"That's a funny way to put it," laughed Bob, "but I know what you mean. And yeah, it *was* hard work, but it sure feels good to know I did it."

Site Visit 8: From Danger To Opportunity                                    81

"No question that you did it," Dr Loring said. "By opening yourself up, you became stronger, but also remember the part your family played in the rebuilding. By trusting them, you let them help you get over some of the difficult obstacles. It may sound funny, but by understanding the steps to rebuilding your house, Bob, I believe you've learned how to lower your stress. We said that *control* was the roof of the house, remember? But control can also be seen as the key to the lock of this House of Seven Cs. By taking charge of the stress-lowering process, you lay claim to that key."

Bob nodded in agreement. "I'm actually less afraid now than I've been in a long time," he offered. "I know it's not going to be easy to find the right job, but I'm prepared now to face that. And you're right. With my family right there beside me, I can face it in a way I never dreamed was possible. Yes, I guess I do know what to do in tough times. Knowing that I'm not alone really makes the difference."

"No one is ever alone," Dr Loring assured him. "All you have to do is find the *courage* to reach out to someone you can trust, and then you can begin to *confront* the issues of stress. By *communicating* your feelings, you begin to take *control* of the situation. The feeling that you're unique in your misery, that no one could possibly understand what you're going through, only adds more stress to what you're already feeling. *Change* is always frightening, Bob, but now you know that you have a *choice* about the way you perceive changes in your life. They can terrify you or they can challenge you. You know, crisis? Will it lead to danger or opportunity? The way you choose to view your situation makes all the difference to your *confidence;* and you need firm and unfaltering confidence, and courage, to help you take the path that will move you ahead in positive ways."

"I think I can make it now, Dr Loring," Bob said. "Thanks to you, I think I'll be okay."

"No, Bob, not thanks to me. Thanks to *you*. I only opened the door to let you in. You had to have the courage to knock on the door and walk through. I didn't make a difference in your life – *you* did. You had to have the desire and the resources to rebuild your emotional house. But remember, if you find yourself starting to backtrack, and you can't recall how to find that key to the lock of the House of Seven Cs, you can always call me. I'll be glad to help you find it again. There is no sense of failure attached to reaching out when you need help, even to a psychologist!"

Bob listened carefully, appreciating what the doctor told him. "I understand that now. In fact, Dr Loring, I've come to see you as a good friend."

The psychologist stood up and held out his hand. "A good friend, yes, but a professional one," he remarked. "In other words, Bob, I'm on the periphery of your life, not in the central core. Your wife and your kids are the ones who are central to you. As long as you can communicate with each other in healthy ways, you'll stay in control. I'm here in case you need some help in stepping back and looking at the problem – getting a new view so you can stay in charge of your life."

Bob shook the psychologist's hand with enthusiasm. "I understand," he said. "And if I feel I need to see you again, I'll call... and believe me, I won't feel guilty about it."

"That's great," Dr Loring said as he opened the office door for Bob for the last time. "Hold on to that key, Bob. As long as you have it firmly in your grasp, your house is storm-proof. It'll take more than an ill wind to blow that house down!"

Bob slung his jacket over his shoulder as he walked through the parking lot to his car. *What a beautiful day it was!* As he opened the car door, he found himself thinking, *What an opportunity Annie and I have to start a new life!*

Bob could hardly wait to get home to Annie and start work on their plans for the future.

## *As we leave the site for the last time, let's take notes in summary*

1. Draw each wall of your house, and write down what you are doing *now* to keep each wall sturdy and strong:
    - communication;
    - confrontation;
    - change;
    - choice.

2. Now look at the roof of your house, and answer these questions about *control*:
    - How are you keeping that roof on?
    - What are you doing, in a proactive way, to keep you in control of your life?

3. Look at your foundation, *confidence,* and the soil *courage,* in which the foundation sits:
    - Each day write down how you're showing *courage,* especially when you get a rejection letter.
    - How are you rebuilding your *confidence?* Think of examples and write them down.

4. Do you feel you have the key to the House of Seven Cs? If not, what is preventing you from having it in your grasp?

# *Final Notes*

ALTHOUGH THIS BOOK DEALS specifically with the trauma of losing a job, it is also a model for coping with any kind of disruption in the life flow. Feelings of grief usually occur when connections are cut, not only in unemployment but in events such as relocation, retirement, divorce and death.

When dramatic change occurs, your emotional house is shaken no matter how firm the foundation. The stability of your emotional house, however, will determine the severity of the aftershock. The important thing to remember is to employ all the tools you have in your house in order to stabilise the situation. Your ability to step back from the crisis and view your own resources, your capacity to confront the situation in its reality and to assess its impact, and your ability to communicate your feelings during difficult times will keep your emotional house from collapsing.

Each part of the house is vital to the rebuilding. Once you get all the parts constructed and are able to nail on the roof, your sense of control will return. When your control is re-established, your house will stand strong and sturdy once again.

Just as in constructing an actual house, rebuilding your emotional house will take time. The more sensitive you are to that aspect, and the more patience you have, the more successful you will be in your own personal reconstruction.

# Final Notes

# Final Notes

# *Congratulations!!!!*

Having read Eileen Berman's excellent book *I'm Fired: A Unique Approach to Rebuilding Your Life* you are well on the way to reconstructing your life and making the most of the opportunities that will come your way.

Why not complete your learning by purchasing the following two books, available at a special price below:

***The Interview Challenge***
Cormac Lankford, 1999, 1-901657-41-8, paperback, £9.99

A practical guide which tells the reader how to be successful at job interviews.

***Work: Inspiration and Transformation***
Andreé Harpur, 1998, 1-901657-22-1, paperback, £9.99

Shows the reader how to choose work that they really enjoy and how to get more out of their working life.

***The Stress Barrier***
Dr Pradeep Chadha, 1999, 1-901657-65-5, paperback, £12.99

A holistic approach to stress management.

All books are available at a special combined price of £20.00, plus £2.00 postage, and can be ordered directly from the publisher, at the address below. Please forward a cheque made out in favour of Blackhall Publishing.

The Order Department
Blackhall Publishing
26 Eustace Street
Dublin 2
Tel: 00-353-1-677-3242
Fax: 00-353-1-677-3243